AS BILL SEES IT

As Bill Sees It

**The A.A. Way of Life...
selected writings
of A.A.'s co-founder**

Alcoholics Anonymous® World Services Inc., New York

AS BILL SEES IT
(formerly THE A.A. WAY OF LIFE)

Copyright © 1967 by

ALCOHOLICS ANONYMOUS ® WORLD SERVICES, INC.

468 Park Avenue South, New York, N.Y.

*Mail address: Box 459, Grand Central Station
New York, NY 10163*

First Printing 1967
Twenty-fifth Printing 1991

ALCOHOLICS ANONYMOUS, A.A. and ⒶⒶ are registered trademarks® of A.A. World Services, In

*This is A.A. General Service
Conference-approved literature*

ISBN 0-916856-03-8
Library of Congress Catalog Card No. 87-402899
PRINTED IN THE UNITED STATES OF AMERICA

Foreword

This volume includes several hundred excerpts from our literature, touching nearly every aspect of A.A.'s way of life. It is felt that this material may become an aid to individual meditation and a stimulant to group discussion, and may well lead to a still wider reading of all our literature.

Over the past twenty-five years, it has been my privilege to write these books about A.A.: the text of "Alcoholics Anonymous," "Twelve Steps and Twelve Traditions," "Alcoholics Anonymous Comes of Age," and "Twelve Concepts for World Service," the last as part of our "Third Legacy Manual." * Many pieces have been written for our monthly magazine, the A.A. Grapevine, and I have always carried on a large personal correspondence.

iii

These are the chief sources from which the content was chosen for this volume. Because the quotations used were lifted out of their original context, it has been necessary in the interest of clarity to edit, and sometimes to rewrite, a number of them.

Of course, all this material reflects my personal viewpoint on A.A.'s way of life. As such, it is bound to have its limitations and imperfections. Nevertheless, one may hope that this new publication will meet a genuine need.

Ever devotedly,

April, 1967

Bill

---

* "*The Third Legacy Manual*" *has been revised and retitled "The A.A. Service Manual." "Twelve Concepts for World Service" was published separately for twelve years but has once again been combined with the manual, beginning with the 1981–82 edition.*

Discussion and Reading Guide

vi

H

Happiness, 29, 53, 57, 69, 163, 216, 218, 233, 249, 254, 298, 302, 306, 321

Hatred; *see* **Anger, Resentment**

Higher Power, 2, 7, 13, 15, 34, 38, 51, 76, 95, 108, 116, 119, 126, 146, 150, 152, 168, 170, 175, 178, 201, 204, 219, 223, 225, 236, 263, 274, 294, 310, 313, 323, 331; agnostics and atheists and, 7, 26, 47, 95, 126, 137, 146, 158, 174, 201, 247, 260, 276, 300, 313, 328; the alcoholic obsession and, 2, 4, 9, 11, 16, 19, 42, 88, 114, 194, 246, 315; A.A. or the group as, 73, 109, 191, 276, 310, 328; reliance on, 26, 33, 55, 66, 72, 78, 87, 93, 104, 117, 122, 129, 139, 155, 200, 206, 210, 221, 239, 249, 265, 293, 319, 329. Also *see* **Faith, Prayer**

Honesty, 17, 20, 44, 52, 70, 74, 83, 102, 140, 141, 156, 172, 173, 205, 213, 222, 227, 238, 248, 251, 258, 277, 279, 295, 312

Humility, need for, 10, 36, 38, 40, 46, 74, 97, 106, 139, 160, 168, 199, 212, 223, 226, 244, 271, 304, 325; ways toward, 2, 12, 31, 44, 83, 91, 106, 126, 149, 156, 159, 191, 211, 213, 236, 246, 248, 291, 305, 311, 316

I

Identification, 24, 195, 212, 228, 231, 252, 257, 302, 303

Illness, alcoholism as an, 4, 27, 32, 35, 45, 88, 118, 121, 130, 141, 180, 194, 217, 218, 257, 283

Inadequacy, 46, 90, 135, 140, 185, 214, 252

Inferiority; *see* **Inadequacy**

Intolerance; *see* **Tolerance**

Inventory, aids to, 10, 17, 33, 39, 80, 89, 96, 111, 132, 142, 144, 193, 205, 213, 215, 222, 248, 258, 261, 267, 270, 279, 281, 289, 296, 301, 303; value of, 10, 12, 17, 54, 64, 65, 68, 106, 111, 140, 149, 161, 164, 173, 216, 233, 261

In page references indicating sources of excerpts, some titles have been abbreviated: A.A. Comes of Age ("Alcoholics Anonymous Comes of Age"); Grapevine (the A.A. Grapevine, our monthly magazine); Service Manual ("The A.A. Service Manual"); Twelve Concepts ("Twelve Concepts for World Service"); Twelve and Twelve ("Twelve Steps and Twelve Traditions"). Two titles appear in full: Alcoholics Anonymous (the Big Book); A.A. Today (the

Progress, A.A. or group, 31, 50, 65, 82, 86, 115, 143, 207, 269, 326. Individual; *see* **Growth**

Public Information, 195, 255, 278, 316

R

Rationalization, 17, 25, 39, 44, 58, 64, 80, 107, 128, 151, 160, 170, 179, 193, 197, 251, 258, 267, 270, 279, 285, 289, 296, 308

Religion; *see* **Higher Power**

Remorse; *see* **Guilt**

Resentment, 5, 39, 56, 58, 98, 176, 179, 268, 286

Responsibility; as an A.A., 9, 13, 32, 50, 57, 79, 84, 125, 229, 255, 271, 290, 297, 307, 317, 319, 331, 332; as an individual, 21, 32, 84, 94, 97, 115, 123, 128, 145, 178, 202, 253, 262, 271, 292, 317. Also *see* **Service, Twelfth-Stepping**

Revenge; *see* **Anger**

S

Sanity, 121, 130, 141. Also *see* **Illness**

Self-Indulgence, 12, 100, 142, 330

Selfishness, 81, 227, 270, 272, 282, 287

Self-Justification; *see* **Rationalization**

Self-Pity, 138, 176, 238, 261, 268, 320

Self-Reliance; *see* **Will**

Self-Righteousness, 17, 28, 38, 107, 170, 181, 183, 274

Self-Satisfaction; *see* **Complacency**

Serenity, 20, 36, 48, 72, 104, 117, 126, 127, 150, 173, 196, 250, 254, 261, 288, 293, 321

Service, 13, 18, 53, 138, 147, 155, 162, 180, 183, 188, 220, 224, 244, 254, 259, 269, 273, 284, 287, 290, 297, 307, 310, 324, 332. Also *see* **Responsibility, Twelfth-Stepping**

Sex, 12, 142, 270, 277, 282

Shortcomings; *see* **Character Defects**

Slips, 11, 52, 68, 99, 154, 184, 197, 213, 214, 251, 291

---

book published by the Grapevine in celebration of A.A.'s twenty-fifth anniversary). The letters and talks by Bill have not been printed before, with two exceptions, for which publication references are given.

AS BILL SEES IT

1

Personality Change

"It has often been said of A.A. that we are interested only in alcoholism. That is not true. We have to get over drinking in order to stay alive. But anyone who knows the alcoholic personality by firsthand contact knows that no true alky ever stops drinking permanently without undergoing a profound personality change."

≪ ≪ ≪   ≫ ≫ ≫

We thought "conditions" drove us to drink, and when we tried to correct these conditions and found that we couldn't do so to our entire satisfaction, our drinking went out of hand and we became alcoholics. It never occurred to us that we needed to change ourselves to meet conditions, whatever they were.

1. LETTER, 1940
2. TWELVE AND TWELVE, P. 47

2

In God's Hands

When we look back, we realize that the things
which came to us when we put ourselves in God's
hands were better than anything we could have
planned.

«« »»

My depression deepened unbearably, and finally
it seemed to me as though I were at the very
bottom of the pit. For the moment, the last
vestige of my proud obstinacy was crushed. All
at once I found myself crying out, "If there is a
God, let Him show Himself! I am ready to do
anything, anything!"

Suddenly the room lit up with a great white light.
It seemed to me, in the mind's eye, that I was
on a mountain and that a wind not of air but of
spirit was blowing. And then it burst upon me
that I was a free man. Slowly the ecstasy sub-
sided. I lay on the bed, but now for a time I was
in another world, a new world of consciousness.
All about me and through me there was a wonderful feeling of Presence, and I thought to myself,
"So this is the God of the preachers!"

1. ALCOHOLICS ANONYMOUS, P. 100
2. A.A. COMES OF AGE, P. 63

3

Pain and Progress

"Years ago I used to commiserate with all people who suffered. Now I commiserate only with those who suffer in ignorance, who do not understand the purpose and ultimate utility of pain."

《《《　》》》

Someone once remarked that pain is the touchstone of spiritual progress. How heartily we A.A.'s can agree with him, for we know that the pains of alcoholism had to come before sobriety, and emotional turmoil before serenity.

《《《　》》》

"Believe more deeply. Hold your face up to the Light, even though for the moment you do not see."

1. LETTER, 1950
2. TWELVE AND TWELVE, PP. 93-94
3. LETTER, 1950

4

Can We Choose?

We must never be blinded by the futile philosophy that we are just the hapless victims of our inheritance, of our life experience, and of our surroundings—that these are the sole forces that make our decisions for us. This is not the road to freedom. We have to believe that we can really choose.

«« »»

"As active alcoholics, we lost our ability to choose whether we would drink. We were the victims of a compulsion which seemed to decree that we must go on with our own destruction.

"Yet we finally did make choices that brought about our recovery. We came to believe that alone we were powerless over alcohol. This was surely a choice, and a most difficult one. We came to believe that a Higher Power could restore us to sanity when we became willing to practice A.A.'s Twelve Steps.

"In short, we chose to 'become willing,' and no better choice did we ever make."

1. GRAPEVINE, NOVEMBER 1960
2. LETTER, 1966

5

Maintenance and Growth

It is plain that a life which includes deep resentment leads only to futility and unhappiness. To the precise extent that we permit these, do we squander the hours that might have been worthwhile. But with the alcoholic, whose hope is the maintenance and growth of a spiritual experience, this business of harboring resentment is infinitely grave. For then we shut ourselves off from the sunlight of the spirit. The insanity of alcohol returns and we drink again. And with us, to drink is to die.

If we were to live, we had to be free of anger. The grouch and the sudden rage were not for us. Anger is the dubious luxury of normal men, but for us alcoholics it is poison.

6

All or Nothing?

Acceptance and faith are capable of producing 100 per cent sobriety. In fact, they usually do; and they must, else we could have no life at all. But the moment we carry these attitudes into our emotional problems, we find that only relative results are possible. Nobody can, for example, become completely free from fear, anger, and pride.

Hence, in this life we shall attain nothing like perfect humility and love. So we shall have to settle, respecting most of our problems, for a very gradual progress, punctuated sometimes by heavy setbacks. Our oldtime attitude of "all or nothing" will have to be abandoned.

7

The Realm of the Spirit

In ancient times material progress was painfully slow. The spirit of modern scientific inquiry, research, and invention was almost unknown.

In the realm of the material, men's minds were fettered by superstition, tradition, and all sorts of fixed ideas. Some of the contemporaries of Columbus thought a round earth preposterous. Others came near putting Galileo to death for his astronomical heresies.

Are not some of us just as biased and unreasonable about the realm of the spirit as were the ancients about the realm of the material?

«‹« ›»›

We have found that God does not make too hard terms with those who seek Him. To us, the realm of spirit is broad, roomy, all inclusive, never exclusive or forbidding to those who earnestly seek. It is open, we believe, to all men.

ALCOHOLICS ANONYMOUS
1. P. 51
2. P. 46

8

A New Life

Is sobriety all that we are to expect of a spiritual awakening? No, sobriety is only a bare beginning; it is only the first gift of the first awakening. If more gifts are to be received, our awakening has to go on. As it does go on, we find that bit by bit we can discard the old life—the one that did not work—for a new life that can and does work under any conditions whatever.

Regardless of worldly success or failure, regardless of pain or joy, regardless of sickness or health or even of death itself, a new life of endless possibilities can be lived if we are willing to continue our awakening, through the practice of A.A.'s Twelve Steps.

GRAPEVINE, DECEMBER 1957

Group and World-Wide Community

The moment Twelfth Step work forms a group, a
discovery is made—that most individuals cannot
recover unless there is a group. Realization dawns
on each member that he is but a small part of a
great whole; that no personal sacrifice is too great
for preservation of the Fellowship. He learns that
the clamor of desires and ambitions within him
must be silenced whenever these could damage
the group.

It becomes plain that the group must survive or
the individual will not.

«‹« »›»

"The Lone member at sea, the A.A. at war in a
far land—all these members know that they belong to A.A.'s world-wide community, that theirs
is only a physical separation, that their fellows
may be as near as the next port of call. Ever so
importantly, they are certain that God's grace is
just as much with them on the high seas or the
lonely outpost as it is with them at home."

1. TWELVE AND TWELVE, P. 130
2. LETTER, 1966

10

Out of the Dark

Self-searching is the means by which we bring
new vision, action, and grace to bear upon the
dark and negative side of our natures. With it
comes the development of that kind of humility
that makes it possible for us to receive God's help.
Yet it is only a step. We will want to go further.

We will want the good that is in us all, even in
the worst of us, to flower and to grow. But first
of all we shall want sunlight; nothing much can
grow in the dark. Meditation is our step out into
the sun.

« « «   » » »

"A clear light seems to fall upon us all—when
we open our eyes. Since our blindness is caused
by our own defects, we must first deeply realize
what they are. Constructive meditation is the first
requirement for each new step in our spiritual
growth."

1. TWELVE AND TWELVE, P. 98
2. LETTER, 1946

11

Quantity or Quality

"About this slip business—I would not be too discouraged. I think you are suffering a great deal from a needless guilt. For some reason or other, the Lord has laid out tougher paths for some of us, and I guess you are treading one of them. God is not asking us to be successful. He is only asking us to try to be. That, you surely are doing, and have been doing. So I would not stay away from A.A. through any feeling of discouragement or shame. It's just the place you should be. Why don't you try just as a member? You don't have to carry the whole A.A. on your back, you know!

"It is not always the quantity of good things that you do, it is also the quality that counts.

"Above all, take it one day at a time."

LETTER, 1958

12

Seeking Fool's Gold

Pride is the basic breeder of most human difficulties, the chief block to true progress. Pride lures us into making demands upon ourselves or upon others which cannot be met without perverting or misusing our God-given instincts. When the satisfaction of our instincts for sex, security, and a place in society becomes the primary object of our lives, then pride steps in to justify our excesses.

«« « » » »

I may attain "humility for today" only to the extent that I am able to avoid the bog of guilt and rebellion on one hand and, on the other hand, that fair but deceiving land which is strewn with the fool's-gold coins of pride. This is how I can find and stay on the highroad to humility, which lies between these extremes. Therefore, a constant inventory which can reveal when I am off the road is always in order.

1. TWELVE AND TWELVE, PP. 48-49
2. GRAPEVINE, JUNE 1961

13

The Shared Gift

A.A. is more than a set of principles; it is a society of alcoholics in action. We must carry the message, else we ourselves can wither and those who haven't been given the truth may die.

《《《　》》》

Faith is more than our greatest gift; its sharing with others is our greatest responsibility. May we of A.A. continually seek the wisdom and the willingness by which we may well fulfill that immense trust which the Giver of all perfect gifts has placed in our hands.

1. SERVICE MANUAL, P. 5
2. GRAPEVINE, APRIL 1961

14

Newcomer Problems

The temptation is to become rather possessive of newcomers. Perhaps we try to give them advice about their affairs which we aren't really competent to give or ought not give at all. Then we are hurt and confused when the advice is rejected, or when it is accepted and brings still greater confusion.

«« »»

"You can't make a horse drink water if he still prefers beer or is too crazy to know what he does want. Set a pail of water beside him, tell him how good it is and why, and leave him alone.

"If people really want to get drunk, there is, so far as I know, no way of stopping this—so leave them alone and let them get drunk. But don't exclude them from the water pail, either."

1. TWELVE AND TWELVE, P. 111
2. LETTER, 1942

15

Eternal Values

Many people will have no truck at all with absolute spiritual values. Perfectionists, they say, are either full of conceit because they fancy they have reached some impossible goal, or else they are swamped in self-condemnation because they have not done so.

Yet I think that we should not hold this view. It is not the fault of great ideals that they are sometimes misused and so become shallow excuses for guilt, rebellion, and pride. On the contrary, we cannot grow very much unless we constantly try to envision what the eternal spiritual values are.

««« »»»

"Day by day, we try to move a little toward God's perfection. So we need not be consumed by maudlin guilt for failure to achieve His likeness and image by Thursday next. Progress is our aim, and His perfection is the beacon, light-years away, that draws us on."

1. GRAPEVINE, JUNE 1961
2. LETTER, 1966

16

Never Again!

"Most people feel more secure on the twenty-four-hour basis than they do in the resolution that they will never drink again. Most of them have broken too many resolutions. It's really a matter of personal choice; every A.A. has the privilege of interpreting the program as he likes.

"Personally, I take the attitude that I intend never to drink again. This is somewhat different from saying, 'I will never drink again.' The latter attitude sometimes gets people in trouble because it is undertaking on a personal basis to do what we alcoholics never could do. It is too much an act of will and leaves too little room for the idea that God will release us from the drink obsession provided we follow the A.A. program."

LETTER, 1949

Toward Honesty

The perverse wish to hide a bad motive underneath a good one permeates human affairs from top to bottom. This subtle and elusive kind of self-righteousness can underlie the smallest act or thought. Learning daily to spot, admit, and correct these flaws is the essence of character-building and good living.

« « «   » » »

The deception of others is nearly always rooted in the deception of ourselves.

« « «   » » »

Somehow, being alone with God doesn't seem as embarrassing as facing up to another person. Until we actually sit down and talk aloud about what we have so long hidden, our willingness to clean house is still largely theoretical. When we are honest with another person, it confirms that we have been honest with ourselves and with God.

1. TWELVE AND TWELVE, PP. 94-95
2. GRAPEVINE, AUGUST 1961
3. TWELVE AND TWELVE, P. 60

18

Companion and Partner

"Dr. Bob was my constant companion and partner
in the great A.A. adventure. As the physician and
great human being that he was, he chose work
with others as his prime A.A. vocation and
achieved a record which, in quantity and in
quality, none will ever surpass. Assisted by the
incomparable Sister Ignatia at St. Thomas Hospital in Akron, he—without charge—medically
treated and spiritually infused five thousand
sufferers.

"In all the stress and strain of A.A.'s pioneering
time, no hard word ever passed between us. For
this, I can thankfully say that the credit was
all his."

《《《   》》》

I took my leave of Dr. Bob, knowing that he was
to undergo a serious operation. The old, broad
smile was on his face as he said almost jokingly,
"Remember, Bill, let's not louse this thing up.
Let's keep it simple!" I turned away, unable to say
a word. That was the last time I ever saw him.

1. LETTER, 1966
2. A.A. COMES OF AGE, P. 214

19

The Wine of Success

Disagreeable or unexpected problems are not the only ones that call for self-control. We must be quite as careful when we begin to achieve some measure of importance and material success. For no people have ever loved personal triumphs more than we have loved them; we drank of success as of a wine which could never fail to make us feel elated. Blinded by prideful self-confidence, we were apt to play the big shot.

Now that we're in A.A. and sober, winning back the esteem of our friends and business associates, we find that we still need to exercise special vigilance. As an insurance against the dangers of big-shot-ism, we can often check ourselves by remembering that we are today sober only by the grace of God and that any success we may be having is far more His success than ours.

20

Light from a Prayer

"God grant us the serenity to accept the things we cannot change, the courage to change the things we can, and the wisdom to know the difference."

《《《　》》》

We treasure our "Serenity Prayer" because it brings a new light to us that can dissipate our oldtime and nearly fatal habit of fooling ourselves.

In the radiance of this prayer we see that defeat, rightly accepted, need be no disaster. We now know that we do not have to run away, nor ought we again try to overcome adversity by still another bulldozing power drive that can only push up obstacles before us faster than they can be taken down.

21

Citizens Again

"Each of us in turn—that is, the member who gets the most out of the program—spends a very large amount of time on Twelfth Step work in the early years. That was my case, and perhaps I should not have stayed sober with less work.

"However, sooner or later most of us are presented with other obligations—to family, friends, and country. As you will remember, the Twelfth Step also refers to 'practicing these principles in all our affairs.' Therefore, I think your choice of whether to take a particular Twelfth Step job is to be found in your own conscience. No one else can tell you for certain what you ought to do at a particular time.

"I just know that you are expected, at some point, to do more than carry the message of A.A. to other alcoholics. In A.A. we aim not only for sobriety—we try again to become citizens of the world that we rejected, and of the world that once rejected us. This is the ultimate demonstration toward which Twelfth Step work is the first but not the final step."

LETTER, 1959

Fear as a Steppingstone

The chief activator of our defects has been self-centered fear—primarily fear that we would lose something we already possessed or would fail to get something we demanded. Living upon a basis of unsatisfied demands, we were in a state of continual disturbance and frustration. Therefore, no peace was to be had unless we could find a means of reducing these demands.

« « «   » » »

For all its usual destructiveness, we have found that fear can be the starting point for better things. Fear can be a steppingstone to prudence and to a decent respect for others. It can point the path to justice, as well as to hate. And the more we have of respect and justice, the more we shall begin to find the love which can suffer much, and yet be freely given. So fear need not always be destructive, because the lessons of its consequences can lead us to positive values.

1. TWELVE AND TWELVE, P. 76
2. GRAPEVINE, JANUARY 1962

Worshipers All

We found that we had indeed been worshipers. What a state of mental goose flesh that used to bring on! Had we not variously worshiped people, sentiment, things, money, and ourselves?

And then, with a better motive, had we not worshipfully beheld the sunset, the sea, or a flower? Who of us had not loved something or somebody? Were not these things the tissue out of which our lives were constructed? Did not these feelings, after all, determine the course of our existence?

It was impossible to say we had no capacity for faith, or love, or worship. In one form or another, we had been living by faith and little else.

Alike When the Chips Are Down

In the beginning, it was four whole years before
A.A. brought permanent sobriety to even one
alcoholic woman. Like the "high bottoms," the
women said they were different; A.A. couldn't
be for them. But as the communication was per-
fected, mostly by the women themselves, the picture changed.

This process of identification and transmission has
gone on and on. The Skid-Rower said he was different. Even more loudly, the socialite (or Park
Avenue stumblebum) said the same—so did the
artists and the professional people, the rich, the
poor, the religious, the agnostic, the Indians and
the Eskimos, the veterans, and the prisoners.

But nowadays all of these, and legions more,
soberly talk about how very much alike all of us
alcoholics are when we admit that the chips are
finally down.

We Cannot Stand Still

In the first days of A.A., I wasn't much bothered about the areas of life in which I was standing still. There was always the alibi: "After all," I said to myself, "I'm far too busy with much more important matters." That was my near perfect prescription for comfort and complacency.

««« »»»

How many of us would presume to declare, "Well, I'm sober and I'm happy. What more can I want, or do? I'm fine the way I am." We know that the price of such self-satisfaction is an inevitable backslide, punctuated at some point by a very rude awakening. We have to grow or else deteriorate. For us, the status quo can only be for today, never for tomorrow. Change we must; we cannot stand still.

1. GRAPEVINE, JUNE 1961
2. GRAPEVINE, FEBRUARY 1961

True Independence of the Spirit

The more we become willing to depend upon a Higher Power, the more independent we actually are. Therefore, dependence as A.A. practices it is really a means of gaining true independence of the spirit.

At the level of everyday living, it is startling to discover how dependent we really are, and how unconscious of that dependence. Every modern house has electric wiring carrying power and light to its interior. By accepting with delight our dependence upon this marvel of science, we find ourselves personally more independent, more comfortable and secure. Power flows just where it is needed. Silently and surely, electricity, that strange energy so few people understand, meets our simplest daily needs.

Though we readily accept this principle of healthy dependence in many of our temporal affairs, we often fiercely resist the identical principle when asked to apply it as a means of growth in the life of the spirit. Clearly, we shall never know freedom under God until we try to seek His will for us. The choice is ours.

TWELVE AND TWELVE, P. 36

Daily Reprieve

We are not cured of alcoholism. What we really have is a daily reprieve contingent on the maintenance of our spiritual condition.

We of A.A. obey spiritual principles, at first because we must, then because we ought to, and ultimately because we love the kind of life such obedience brings. Great suffering and great love are A.A.'s disciplinarians; we need no others.

1. ALCOHOLICS ANONYMOUS, P. 85
2. TWELVE AND TWELVE, P. 174

Troublemakers Can Be Teachers

Few of us are any longer afraid of what any new-comer can do to our A.A. reputation or effectiveness. Those who slip, those who panhandle, those who scandalize, those with mental twists, those who rebel at the program, those who trade on the A.A. reputation—all such persons seldom harm an A.A. group for long.

Some of these have become our most respected and best loved. Some have remained to try our patience, sober nevertheless. Others have drifted away. We have begun to regard the troublesome ones not as menaces, but rather as our teachers. They oblige us to cultivate patience, tolerance, and humility. We finally see that they are only people sicker than the rest of us, that we who condemn them are the Pharisees whose false righteousness does our group the deeper spiritual damage.

Gratitude Should Go Forward

"Gratitude should go forward, rather than backward.

"In other words, if you carry the message to still others, you will be making the best possible repayment for the help given to you."

«« » »

No satisfaction has been deeper and no joy greater than in a Twelfth Step job well done. To watch the eyes of men and women open with wonder as they move from darkness into light, to see their lives quickly fill with new purpose and meaning, and above all to watch them awaken to the presence of a loving God in their lives—these things are the substance of what we receive as we carry A.A.'s message.

1. LETTER, 1959
2. TWELVE AND TWELVE, P. 110

Getting off a "Dry Bender"

"Sometimes, we become depressed. I ought to know; I have been a champion dry-bender case myself. While the surface causes were a part of the picture—trigger-events that precipitated depression—the underlying causes, I am satisfied, ran much deeper.

"Intellectually, I could accept my situation. Emotionally, I could not.

"To these problems, there are certainly no pat answers. But part of the answer surely lies in the constant effort to practice all of A.A.'s Twelve Steps."

LETTER, 1954

31

In God's Economy

"In God's economy, nothing is wasted. Through failure, we learn a lesson in humility which is probably needed, painful though it is."

We did not always come closer to wisdom by reason of our virtues; our better understanding is often rooted in the pains of our former follies. Because this has been the essence of our individual experience, it is also the essence of our experience as a fellowship.

1. LETTER, 1942
2. GRAPEVINE, NOVEMBER 1961

32

Moral Responsibility

"Some strongly object to the A.A. position that alcoholism is an illness. This concept, they feel, removes moral responsibility from alcoholics. As any A.A. knows, this is far from true. We do not use the concept of sickness to absolve our members from responsibility. On the contrary, we use the fact of fatal illness to clamp the heaviest kind of moral obligation onto the sufferer, the obligation to use A.A.'s Twelve Steps to get well.

"In the early days of his drinking, the alcoholic is often guilty of irresponsibility. But once the time of compulsive drinking has arrived, he can't very well be held fully accountable for his conduct. He then has an obsession that condemns him to drink, and a bodily sensitivity to alcohol that guarantees his final madness and death.

"But when he is made aware of this condition, he is under pressure to accept A.A.'s program of moral regeneration."

TALK, 1960

33

Foundation for Life

We discover that we receive guidance for our lives to just about the extent that we stop making demands upon God to give it to us on order and on our terms.

《《《   》》》

In praying, we ask simply that throughout the day God place in us the best understanding of His will that we can have for that day, and that we be given the grace by which we may carry it out.

《《《   》》》

There is a direct linkage among self-examination, meditation, and prayer. Taken separately, these practices can bring much relief and benefit. But when they are logically related and interwoven, the result is an unshakable foundation for life.

TWELVE AND TWELVE
1. p. 104
2. p. 102
3. p. 98

"Not Allied with Any Sect . . ."

"While A.A. has restored thousands of poor Christians to their churches, and has made believers out of atheists and agnostics, it has also made good A.A.'s out of those belonging to the Buddhist, Islamic, and Jewish faiths. For example, we question very much whether our Buddhist members in Japan would ever have joined this Society had A.A. officially stamped itself a strictly Christian movement.

"You can easily convince yourself of this by imagining that A.A. started among the Buddhists and that they then told you you couldn't join them unless you became a Buddhist, too. If you were a Christian alcoholic under these circumstances, you might well turn your face to the wall and die."

LETTER, 1954

Suffering Transmuted

"A.A. is no success story in the ordinary sense of the word. It is a story of suffering transmuted, under grace, into spiritual progress."

《《《　》》》

For Dr. Bob, the insatiable craving for alcohol was evidently a physical phenomenon which bedeviled several of his first years in A.A., a time when only days and nights of carrying the message to other alcoholics could cause him to forget about drinking. Although his craving was hard to withstand, it doubtless did account for some part of the intense incentive that went into forming Akron's Group Number One.

Bob's spiritual release did not come easily; it was to be painfully slow. It always entailed the hardest kind of work and the sharpest vigilance.

1. LETTER, 1959
2. A.A. COMES OF AGE, P. 69

Humility First

We found many in A.A. who once thought, as we did, that humility was another name for weakness. They helped us to get down to our right size. By their example they showed us that humility and intellect could be compatible, provided we placed humility first. When we began to do that, we received the gift of faith, a faith which works. This faith is for you, too.

《《《　》》》

Where humility formerly stood for a forced feeding on humble pie, it now begins to mean the nourishing ingredient that can give us serenity.

TWELVE AND TWELVE
1. p. 30
2. p. 74

A Full and Thankful Heart

One exercise that I practice is to try for a full inventory of my blessings and then for a right acceptance of the many gifts that are mine—both temporal and spiritual. Here I try to achieve a state of joyful gratitude. When such a brand of gratitude is repeatedly affirmed and pondered, it can finally displace the natural tendency to congratulate myself on whatever progress I may have been enabled to make in some areas of living.

I try hard to hold fast to the truth that a full and thankful heart cannot entertain great conceits. When brimming with gratitude, one's heartbeat must surely result in outgoing love, the finest emotion that we can ever know.

Pipeline to God

"I am a firm believer in both guidance and prayer. But I am fully aware, and humble enough, I hope, to see there may be nothing infallible about my guidance.

"The minute I figure I have got a perfectly clear pipeline to God, I have become egotistical enough to get into real trouble. Nobody can cause more needless grief than a power-driver who thinks he has got it straight from God."

LETTER, 1950

Dealing with Resentments

Resentment is the Number One offender. It destroys more alcoholics than anything else. From it stem all forms of spiritual disease, for we have been not only mentally and physically ill, we have also been spiritually ill. When our spiritual malady is overcome, we straighten out mentally and physically.

In dealing with our resentments, we set them on paper. We listed people, institutions, or principles with whom we were angry. We asked ourselves why we were angry. In most cases it was found that our self-esteem, our pocketbooks, our ambitions, our personal relationships (including sex) were hurt or threatened.

«« »»

"The most heated bit of letter-writing can be a wonderful safety valve—providing the wastebasket is somewhere nearby."

1. ALCOHOLICS ANONYMOUS, PP. 64-65
2. LETTER, 1949

40

Material Achievement

No member of A.A. wants to deprecate material achievement. Nor do we enter into debate with the many who cling to the belief that to satisfy our basic natural desires is the main object of life. But we are sure that no class of people in the world ever made a worse mess of trying to live by this formula than alcoholics.

We demanded more than our share of security, prestige, and romance. When we seemed to be succeeding, we drank to dream still greater dreams. When we were frustrated, even in part, we drank for oblivion.

In all these strivings, so many of them well-intentioned, our crippling handicap was our lack of humility. We lacked the perspective to see that character-building and spiritual values had to come first, and that material satisfactions were simply by-products and not the chief aims of life.

41

Membership Rules?

Around 1943 or 1944, the Central Office asked
the groups to list their membership rules and
send them in. After they arrived we set them all
down. A little reflection upon these many rules
brought us to an astonishing conclusion.

If all of these edicts had been in force everywhere
at once it would have been practically impossible
for any alcoholic to have ever joined A.A. About
nine-tenths of our oldest and best members could
never have got by!

«« »»

At last experience taught us that to take away
any alcoholic's full chance for sobriety in A.A.
was sometimes to pronounce his death sentence,
and often to condemn him to endless misery. Who
dared to be judge, jury, and executioner of his own
sick brother?

1. GRAPEVINE, AUGUST 1946
2. TWELVE AND TWELVE, P. 141

Self-Confidence and Will Power

When first challenged to admit defeat, most of us revolted. We had approached A.A. expecting to be taught self-confidence. Then we had been told that so far as alcohol was concerned, self-confidence was no good whatever; in fact, it was a total liability. There was no such thing as personal conquest of the alcoholic compulsion by the unaided will.

«« »»

It is when we try to make our will conform with God's that we begin to use it rightly. To all of us, this was a most wonderful revelation. Our whole trouble had been the misuse of will power. We had tried to bombard our problems with it instead of attempting to bring it into agreement with God's intention for us. To make this increasingly possible is the purpose of A.A.'s Twelve Steps.

TWELVE AND TWELVE
1. P. 22
2. P. 40

43

How Much Anonymity?

As a rule, the average newcomer wanted his family to know immediately what he was trying to do. He also wanted to tell others who had tried to help him—his doctor, his minister, and close friends. As he gained confidence, he felt it right to explain his new way of life to his employer and business associates. When opportunities to be helpful came along, he found he could talk easily about A.A. to almost anyone.

These quiet disclosures helped him to lose his fear of the alcoholic stigma, and spread the news of A.A.'s existence in his community. Many a new man and woman came to A.A. because of such conversations. Since it is only at the top public level that anonymity is expected, such communications were well within its spirit.

TWELVE AND TWELVE, PP. 185-186

Daily Acceptance

"Too much of my life has been spent in dwelling upon the faults of others. This is a most subtle and perverse form of self-satisfaction, which permits us to remain comfortably unaware of our own defects. Too often we are heard to say, 'If it weren't for him (or her), how happy I'd be!' "

« « «   » » »

Our very first problem is to accept our present circumstances as they are, ourselves as we are, and the people about us as they are. This is to adopt a realistic humility without which no genuine advance can even begin. Again and again, we shall need to return to that unflattering point of departure. This is an exercise in acceptance that we can profitably practice every day of our lives.

Provided we strenuously avoid turning these realistic surveys of the facts of life into unrealistic alibis for apathy or defeatism, they can be the sure foundation upon which increased emotional health and therefore spiritual progress can be built.

1. LETTER, 1966
2. GRAPEVINE, MARCH 1962

45

Our Companions

Today, the vast majority of us welcome any new light that can be thrown on the alcoholic's mysterious and baffling malady. We welcome new and valuable knowledge whether it issues from a test tube, from a psychiatrist's couch, or from revealing social studies. We are glad of any kind of education that accurately informs the public and changes its age-old attitude toward the drunk.

More and more we regard all who labor in the total field of alcoholism as our companions on a march from darkness into light. We see that we can accomplish together what we could never accomplish in separation and in rivalry.

GRAPEVINE, MARCH 1958

46

True Ambition—and False

We have had a much keener look at ourselves and those about us. We have seen that we were prodded by unreasonable fears or anxieties into making a life business of winning fame, money, and what we thought was leadership. So false pride became the reverse side of that ruinous coin marked "Fear." We simply had to be Number One people to cover up our deep-lying inferiorities.

True ambition is not what we thought it was. True ambition is the profound desire to live usefully and walk humbly under the grace of God.

TWELVE AND TWELVE
1. p. 123
2. pp. 124-125

Seeing Is Believing

The Wright brothers' almost childish faith that they could build a machine which would fly was the mainspring of their accomplishment. Without that, nothing could have happened.

We agnostics and atheists were sticking to the idea that self-sufficiency would solve our problems. When others showed us that God-sufficiency worked with them, we began to feel like those who had insisted the Wrights would never fly. We were seeing another kind of flight, a spiritual liberation from this world, people who rose above their problems.

ALCOHOLICS ANONYMOUS, PP. 52-53, 55

48

Live Serenely

When a drunk has a terrific hangover because he drank heavily yesterday, he cannot live well today. But there is another kind of hangover which we all experience whether we are drinking or not. That is the emotional hangover, the direct result of yesterday's and sometimes today's excesses of negative emotion—anger, fear, jealousy, and the like.

If we would live serenely today and tomorrow, we certainly need to eliminate these hangovers. This doesn't mean we need to wander morbidly around in the past. It requires an admission and correction of errors—now.

TWELVE AND TWELVE, PP. 88-89

Out of Defeat . . . Strength

If we are planning to stop drinking, there must be no reservation of any kind, nor any lurking notion that some day we will be immune to alcohol.

« « «   » » »

Such is the paradox of A.A. regeneration: strength arising out of complete defeat and weakness, the loss of one's old life as a condition for finding a new one.

1. ALCOHOLICS ANONYMOUS, P. 33
2. A.A. COMES OF AGE, P. 46

A.A.: Benign Anarchy and Democracy

When we come into A.A. we find a greater personal freedom than any other society knows. We cannot be compelled to do anything. In that sense our Society is a benign anarchy. The word "anarchy" has a bad meaning to most of us. But I think that the idealist who first advocated the concept felt that if only men were granted absolute liberty, and were compelled to obey no one, they would then voluntarily associate themselves in the common interest. A.A. is an association of the benign sort he envisioned.

But when we had to go into action—to function as groups—we discovered that we also had to become a democracy. As our oldtimers retired, we therefore began to elect our trusted servants by majority vote. Each group in this sense became a town meeting. All plans for group action had to be approved by the majority. This meant that no single individual could appoint himself to act for his group or for A.A. as a whole. Neither dictatorship nor paternalism was for us.

A.A. COMES OF AGE, PP. 224-225

The Coming of Faith

In my own case, the foundation stone of freedom
from fear is that of faith: a faith that, despite all
worldly appearances to the contrary, causes me to
believe that I live in a universe that makes sense.

To me, this means a belief in a Creator who is
all power, justice, and love; a God who intends
for me a purpose, a meaning, and a destiny to
grow, however little and haltingly, toward His own
likeness and image. Before the coming of faith I
had lived as an alien in a cosmos that too often
seemed both hostile and cruel. In it there could be
no inner security for me.

« « «   » » »

"When I was driven to my knees by alcohol, I
was made ready to ask for the gift of faith. And
all was changed. Never again, my pains and problems notwithstanding, would I experience my
former desolation. I saw the universe to be
lighted by God's love; I was alone no more."

1. GRAPEVINE, JANUARY 1962
2. LETTER, 1966

52

To Guard Against a Slip

Suppose we fall short of our chosen ideals and stumble? Does this mean we are going to get drunk? Some people tell us so. But this is only a half-truth.

It depends on us and on our motives. If we are sorry for what we have done, and have the honest desire to let God take us to better things, we believe we will be forgiven and will have learned our lesson. If we are not sorry, and our conduct continues to harm others, we are quite sure to drink. These are facts out of our experience.

53

"Loners"—but Not Alone

What can be said of many A.A. members who, for a variety of reasons, cannot have a family life? At first many of these feel lonely, hurt, and left out as they witness so much domestic happiness about them. If they cannot have this kind of happiness, can A.A. offer them satisfactions of similar worth and durability?

Yes—whenever they try hard to seek out these satisfactions. Surrounded by so many A.A. friends, the so-called loners tell us they no longer feel alone. In partnership with others—women and men—they can devote themselves to any number of ideas, people, and constructive projects. They can participate in enterprises which would be denied to family men and women. We daily see such members render prodigies of service, and receive great joys in return.

54

To Deepen Our Insight

It is necessary that we extricate from an examination of our personal relations every bit of information about ourselves and our fundamental difficulties that we can. Since defective relations with other human beings have nearly always been the immediate cause of our woes, including our alcoholism, no field of investigation could yield more satisfying and valuable rewards than this one.

Calm, thoughtful reflection upon personal relations can deepen our insight. We can go far beyond those things which were superficially wrong with us, to see those flaws which were basic, flaws which sometimes were responsible for the whole pattern of our lives. Thoroughness, we have found, will pay—and pay handsomely.

Seeking Guidance

"Man is supposed to think, and act. He wasn't made in God's image to be an automaton.

"My own formula along this line runs as follows: First, think through every situation pro and con, praying meanwhile that I be not influenced by ego considerations. Affirm that I would like to do God's will.

"Then, having turned the problem over in this fashion and getting no conclusive or compelling answer, I wait for further guidance, which may come into the mind directly or through other people or through circumstances.

"If I feel I can't wait, and still get no definite indication, I repeat the first measure several times, try to pick out the best course, and then proceed to act. I know if I am wrong, the heavens won't fall. A lesson will be learned, in any case."

LETTER, 1950

Facing Criticism

Sometimes, we register surprise, shock, and anger when people find fault with A.A. We are apt to be disturbed to such an extent that we cannot benefit by constructive criticism.

This sort of resentment makes no friends and achieves no constructive purpose. Certainly, this is an area in which we can improve.

«« »»

It is evident that the harmony, security, and future effectiveness of A.A. will depend largely upon our maintenance of a thoroughly nonaggressive and pacific attitude in all our public relations. This is an exacting assignment, because in our drinking days we were prone to anger, hostility, rebellion, and aggression. And, even though we are now sober, the old patterns of behavior are to a degree still with us, always threatening to explode on any good excuse.

But we now know this, and therefore I feel confident that in the conduct of our public affairs we shall always find the grace to exert restraint.

1. GRAPEVINE, JULY 1965
2. TWELVE CONCEPTS, P. 68

Better than Gold

As newcomers, many of us have indulged in spiritual intoxication. Like a gaunt prospector, belt drawn in over the last ounce of food, we saw our pick strike gold. Joy at our release from a lifetime of frustration knew no bounds.

The newcomer feels he has struck something better than gold. He may not see at once that he has barely scratched a limitless lode which will pay dividends only if he mines it for the rest of his life and insists on giving away the entire product.

ALCOHOLICS ANONYMOUS, pp. 128-129

Righteous Indignation

"The positive value of righteous indignation is theoretical—especially for alcoholics. It leaves every one of us open to the rationalization that we may be as angry as we like provided we can claim to be righteous about it."

«‹«   »›»

When we harbored grudges and planned revenge for defeats, we were really beating ourselves with the club of anger we had intended to use on others. We learned that if we were seriously disturbed, our very first need was to quiet that disturbance, regardless of who or what we thought caused it.

1. LETTER, 1954
2. TWELVE AND TWELVE, P. 47

59

Conviction and Compromise

One qualification for a useful life is give-and-take, the ability to compromise cheerfully. Compromise comes hard to us "all or nothing" drunks. Nevertheless, we must never lose sight of the fact that progress is nearly always characterized by a series of improving compromises.

Of course, we cannot always compromise. There are circumstances in which it is necessary to stick flat-footed to one's convictions until the issue is resolved. Deciding when to compromise and when not to compromise always calls for the most careful discrimination.

TWELVE CONCEPTS, PP. 39–40

60

Brain Power Alone?

To the intellectually self-sufficient man or woman, many A.A.'s can say, "Yes, we were like you— far too smart for our own good. We loved to have people call us precocious. We used our education to blow ourselves up into prideful balloons, though we were careful to hide this from others. Secretly, we felt we could float above the rest of the folks on our brain power alone.

"Scientific progress told us there was nothing man couldn't do. Knowledge was all powerful. Intellect could conquer nature. Since we were brighter than most folks (so we thought), the spoils of victory would be ours for the thinking. The god of intellect displaced the God of our fathers.

"But John Barleycorn had other ideas. We who had won so handsomely in a walk turned into all-time losers. We saw that we had to reconsider or die."

TWELVE AND TWELVE, PP. 29-30

61

Resolving Fear

Fear somehow touched about every aspect of our
lives. It was an evil and corroding thread; the
fabric of our existence was shot through with it.
It set in motion trains of circumstances which
brought us misfortune we felt we didn't deserve.
But did not we often set the ball rolling ourselves?

« « «   » » »

The problem of resolving fear has two aspects.
We shall have to try for all the freedom from fear
that is possible for us to attain. Then we shall
need to find both the courage and the grace to
deal constructively with whatever fears remain.

1. ALCOHOLICS ANONYMOUS, PP. 67-68
2. GRAPEVINE, JANUARY 1962

62

A Different Swinging Door

When a drunk shows up among us and says that he doesn't like the A.A. principles, people, or service management, when he declares that he can do better elsewhere—we are not worried. We simply say, "Maybe your case really is different. Why don't you try something else?"

If an A.A. member says he doesn't like his own group, we are not disturbed. We simply say, "Why don't you try another one? Or start one of your own."

To those who wish to secede from A.A. altogether, we extend a cheerful invitation to do just that. If they can do better by other means, we are glad. If after a trial they cannot do better, we know they face a choice: They can go mad or die or they can return to A.A. The decision is wholly theirs. (As a matter of fact, most of them do come back.)

TWELVE CONCEPTS, P. 72

Free of Dependence

I asked myself, "Why can't the Twelve Steps work to release me from this unbearable depression?" By the hour, I stared at the St. Francis Prayer: "It is better to comfort than to be comforted."

Suddenly I realized what the answer might be. My basic flaw had always been dependence on people or circumstances to supply me with prestige, security, and confidence. Failing to get these things according to my perfectionist dreams and specifications, I fought for them. And when defeat came, so did my depression.

Reinforced by what grace I could find in prayer, I had to exert every ounce of will and action to cut off these faulty emotional dependencies upon people and upon circumstances. Then only could I be free to love as Francis had loved.

64

Search for Motives

Some of us clung to the claim that when drinking we never hurt anybody but ourselves. Our families didn't suffer, because we always paid the bills and seldom drank at home. Our business associates didn't suffer, because we were usually on the job. Our reputations didn't suffer, because we were certain few knew of our drinking. Those who did would sometimes assure us that, after all, a lively bender was only a good man's fault. What real harm, therefore, had we done? No more, surely, than we could easily mend with a few casual apologies.

This attitude, of course, is the end result of purposeful forgetting. It is an attitude which can be changed only by a deep and honest search of our motives and actions.

65

Growth by the Tenth Step

In the years ahead A.A. will, of course, make mistakes. Experience has taught us that we need have no fear of doing this, providing that we always remain willing to admit our faults and to correct them promptly. Our growth as individuals has depended upon this healthy process of trial and error. So will our growth as a fellowship.

Let us always remember that any society of men and women that cannot freely correct its own faults must surely fall into decay if not into collapse. Such is the universal penalty for the failure to go on growing. Just as each A.A. must continue to take his moral inventory and act upon it, so must our whole Society if we are to survive and if we are to serve usefully and well.

For Emergencies Only?

Whether we had been believers or unbelievers, we began to get over the idea that the Higher Power was a sort of bush-league pinch hitter, to be called upon only in an emergency.

The notion that we would still live our own lives, God helping a little now and then, began to evaporate. Many of us who had thought ourselves religious awoke to the limitations of this attitude. Refusing to place God first, we had deprived ourselves of His help.

But now the words "Of myself I am nothing, the Father doeth the works" began to carry bright promise and meaning.

Thousands of "Founders"

"While I thank God that I was privileged to be an early member of A.A., I honestly wish that the word 'founder' could be eliminated from the A.A. vocabulary.

"When you get right down to it, everyone who has done any amount of successful Twelfth Step work is bound to be the founder of a new life for other alcoholics."

《 《 《   》 》 》

"A.A. was not invented! Its basics were brought to us through the experience and wisdom of many great friends. We simply borrowed and adapted their ideas."

《 《 《   》 》 》

"Thankfully, we have accepted the devoted services of many nonalcoholics. We owe our very lives to the men and women of medicine and religion. And, speaking for Dr. Bob and myself, I gratefully declare that had it not been for our wives, Anne and Lois, neither of us could have lived to see A.A.'s beginning."

1. LETTER, 1945
2. LETTER, 1966
3. LETTER, 1966

Renew Your Effort

"Though I know how hurt and sorry you must be after this slip, please do not worry about a temporary loss of your inner peace. As calmly as you can, just renew your effort on the A.A. program, especially those parts of it which have to do with meditation and self-analysis.

"Could I also suggest that you look at excessive guilt for what it is? Nothing but a sort of reverse pride. A decent regret for what has happened is fine. But guilt—no.

"Indeed, the slip could well have been brought about by unreasonable feelings of guilt because of other moral failures, so called. Surely, you ought to look into this possibility. Even here you should not blame yourself for failure; you can be penalized only for refusing to try for better things."

LETTER, 1958

Giving Without Demand

Watch any A.A. of six months working with a Twelfth Step prospect. If the newcomer says, "To the devil with you," the twelfth-stepper only smiles and finds another alcoholic to help. He doesn't feel frustrated or rejected. If his next drunk responds, and in turn starts to give love and attention to other sufferers, yet gives none back to him, the sponsor is happy about it anyway. He still doesn't feel rejected; instead he rejoices that his former prospect is sober and happy.

And he well knows that his own life has been made richer, as an extra dividend of giving to another without any demand for a return.

Truth, the Liberator

How truth makes us free is something that we
A.A.'s can well understand. It cut the shackles
that once bound us to alcohol. It continues to release us from conflicts and miseries beyond
reckoning; it banishes fear and isolation. The
unity of our Fellowship, the love we cherish for
each other, the esteem in which the world holds
us—all of these are products of the truth which,
under God, we have been privileged to perceive.

«·«·«   »·»·»

Just how and when we tell the truth—or keep
silent—can often reveal the difference between
genuine integrity and none at all.

Step Nine emphatically cautions us against misusing the truth when it states: "We made direct
amends to such people wherever possible, except
when to do so would injure them or others." Because it points up the fact that the truth can be
used to injure as well as to heal, this valuable
principle certainly has a wide-ranging application
to the problem of developing integrity.

GRAPEVINE, AUGUST 1961

"How Can You Roll with a Punch?"

On the day that the calamity of Pearl Harbor fell
upon our country, a great friend of A.A. was walking along a St. Louis street. Father Edward
Dowling was not an alcoholic, but he had been
one of the founders of the struggling A.A.
group in his city. Because many of his usually
sober friends had already taken to their bottles
that they might blot out the implications of the
Pearl Harbor disaster, Father Ed was anguished
by the thought that his cherished A.A. group
would probably do the same.

Then a member, sober less than a year, stepped
alongside and engaged Father Ed in a spirited conversation—mostly about A.A. Father Ed saw,
with relief, that his companion was perfectly sober.

"How is it that you have nothing to say about
Pearl Harbor? How can you roll with a punch like
that?"

"Well," replied the yearling, "each of us in A.A.
has already had his own private Pearl Harbor. So
why should we drunks crack up over this one?"

Dependence—Unhealthy or Healthy

"Nothing can be more demoralizing than a clinging and abject dependence upon another human being. This often amounts to the demand for a degree of protection and love that no one could possibly satisfy. So our hoped-for protectors finally flee, and once more we are left alone—either to grow up or to disintegrate."

《《《　》》》

We discovered the best possible source of emotional stability to be God Himself. We found that dependence upon His perfect justice, forgiveness, and love was healthy, and that it would work where nothing else would.

If we really depended upon God, we couldn't very well play God to our fellows, nor would we feel the urge to rely wholly on human protection and care.

1. LETTER, 1966
2. TWELVE AND TWELVE, P. 116

Two-Way Tolerance

"Your point of view was once mine. Fortunately, A.A. is constructed so that we need not debate the existence of God; but for best results, most of us must depend upon a Higher Power. You say the group is your Higher Power, and no right-minded A.A. would challenge your privilege to believe precisely that way. We should all be glad that good recoveries can be made even on this limited basis.

"But turnabout is fair play. If you would expect tolerance for your point of view, I am sure you would be willing to reciprocate. I try to remember that, down through the centuries, lots of brighter people than I have been found on both sides of this debate about belief. For myself, of late years, I am finding it much easier to believe that God made man, than that man made God."

LETTER, 1950

Breach the Walls of Ego

People who are driven by pride of self unconsciously blind themselves to their liabilities. Newcomers of this sort scarcely need comforting. The
problem is to help them discover a chink in the
walls their ego has built, through which the light
of reason can shine.

《 《 《　 》 》 》

The attainment of greater humility is the foundation principle of each of A.A.'s Twelve Steps. For
without some degree of humility, no alcoholic can
stay sober at all.

Nearly all A.A.'s have found, too, that unless they
develop much more of this precious quality than
may be required just for sobriety, they still haven't
much chance of becoming truly happy. Without it,
they cannot live to much useful purpose, or, in
adversity, be able to summon the faith that can
meet any emergency.

TWELVE AND TWELVE
1. p. 46
2. p. 70

Losing Financial Fears

When a job still looked like a mere means of getting money rather than an opportunity for service, when the acquisition of money for financial independence looked more important than a right dependence upon God, we were the victims of unreasonable fears. And these were fears which would make a serene and useful existence, at any financial level, quite impossible.

But as time passed we found that with the help of A.A.'s Twelve Steps we could lose those fears, no matter what our material prospects were. We could cheerfully perform humble labor without worrying about tomorrow. If our circumstances happened to be good, we no longer dreaded a change for the worse, for we had learned that these troubles could be turned into great values, for ourselves and for others.

TWELVE AND TWELVE, PP. 121-122

76

Only God Is Unchanging

"Change is the characteristic of all growth. From drinking to sobriety, from dishonesty to honesty, from conflict to serenity, from hate to love, from childish dependence to adult responsibility—all this and infinitely more represent change for the better.

"Such changes are accomplished by a belief in and a practice of sound principles. Here we must needs discard bad or ineffective principles in favor of good ones that work. Even good principles can sometimes be displaced by the discovery of still better ones.

"Only God is unchanging; only He has all the truth there is."

LETTER, 1966

R.S.V.P.—Yes or No?

Usually, we do not avoid a place where there is drinking—if we have a legitimate reason for being there. That includes bars, night clubs, dances, receptions, weddings, even plain ordinary parties.

You will note that we made an important qualification. Therefore, ask yourself, "Have I any good social, business, or personal reason for going to this place? Or am I expecting to steal a little vicarious pleasure from the atmosphere?" Then go or stay away, whichever seems better. But be sure you are on solid spiritual ground before you start and that your motive in going is thoroughly good. Do not think of what you will get out of the occasion. Think of what you can bring to it.

If you are shaky, you had better work with another alcoholic instead!

Clearing a Channel

During the day, we can pause where situations must be met and decisions made, and renew the simple request "Thy will, not mine, be done."

If at these points our emotional disturbance happens to be great, we will more surely keep our balance provided we remember, and repeat to ourselves, a particular prayer or phrase that has appealed to us in our reading or meditation. Just saying it over and over will often enable us to clear a channel choked up with anger, fear, frustration, or misunderstanding, and permit us to return to the surest help of all—our search for God's will, not our own, in the moment of stress.

Whose Responsibility?

"An A.A. group, as such, cannot take on all the personal problems of its members, let alone those of nonalcoholics in the world around us. The A.A. group is not, for example, a mediator of domestic relations, nor does it furnish personal financial aid to anyone.

"Though a member may sometimes be helped in such matters by his friends in A.A., the primary responsibility for the solutions of all his problems of living and growing rests squarely upon the individual himself. Should an A.A. group attempt this sort of help, its effectiveness and energies would be hopelessly dissipated.

"This is why sobriety—freedom from alcohol—through the teaching and practice of A.A.'s Twelve Steps, is the sole purpose of the group. If we don't stick to this cardinal principle, we shall almost certainly collapse. And if we collapse we cannot help anyone."

LETTER, 1966

Debits and Credits

Following a gossip binge, we can well ask ourselves these questions: "Why did we say what we did? Were we only trying to be helpful and informative? Or were we not trying to feel superior by confessing the other fellow's sins? Or, because of fear and dislike, were we not really aiming to damage him?"

This would be an honest attempt to examine ourselves, rather than the other fellow.

«««   »»»

Inventory-taking is not always done in red ink. It's a poor day indeed when we haven't done something right. As a matter of fact, the waking hours are usually well filled with things that are constructive. Good intentions, good thoughts, and good acts are there for us to see.

Even when we have tried hard and failed, we may chalk that up as one of the greatest credits of all.

1. GRAPEVINE, AUGUST 1961
2. TWELVE AND TWELVE, P. 93

"Selfish"?

"I can see why you are disturbed to hear some A.A. speakers say, 'A.A. is a selfish program.' The word 'selfish' ordinarily implies that one is acquisitive, demanding, and thoughtless of the welfare of others. Of course, the A.A. way of life does not at all imply such undesirable traits.

"What do these speakers mean? Well, any theologian will tell you that the salvation of his own soul is the highest vocation that a man can have. Without salvation—however we may define this—he will have little or nothing. For us of A.A., there is even more urgency.

"If we cannot or will not achieve sobriety, then we become truly lost, right in the here and now. We are of no value to anyone, including ourselves, until we find salvation from alcohol. Therefore, our own recovery and spiritual growth have to come first—a right and necessary kind of self-concern."

LETTER, 1966

82

Trouble Becomes an Asset

"I think that this particular General Service Conference holds promise and has been filled with progress—because it has had trouble. And it has converted that trouble into an asset, into some growth, and into a great promise.

"A.A. was born out of trouble, one of the most serious kinds of trouble that can befall an individual, the trouble attendant upon this dark and fatal malady of alcoholism. Every single one of us approached A.A. in trouble, in impossible trouble, in hopeless trouble. And that is why we came.

"If this Conference was ruffled, if individuals were deeply disturbed—I say, 'This is fine.' What parliament, what republic, what democracy has not been disturbed? Friction of opposing viewpoints is the very modus operandi on which they proceed. Then what should we be afraid of?"

TALK, 1958

We Cannot Live Alone

All of A.A.'s Twelve Steps ask us to go contrary
to our natural desires; they all deflate our egos.
When it comes to ego deflation, few Steps are
harder to take than the Fifth. Scarcely any Step is
more necessary to long-time sobriety and peace of
mind.

A.A. experience has taught us we cannot live
alone with our pressing problems and the character defects which cause or aggravate them. If
Step Four has revealed in stark relief those
experiences we'd rather not remember, then the
need to quit living by ourselves with those
tormenting ghosts of yesterday gets more urgent
than ever. We have to talk to somebody about
them.

«« «   » »»

We cannot wholly rely on friends to solve all our
difficulties. A good adviser will never do all our
thinking for us. He knows that each final choice
must be ours. He will therefore help to eliminate
fear, expediency, and self-deception, so enabling
us to make choices which are loving, wise, and
honest.

1. TWELVE AND TWELVE, P. 55
2. GRAPEVINE, AUGUST 1961

Benefits of Responsibility

"Happily, A.A.'s per capita expenses are very low. For us to fail to meet them would be to evade a responsibility beneficial for us.

"Most alcoholics have said they had no troubles that money would not cure. We are a group that, when drinking, always held out a hand for funds. So when we commence to pay our own service bills, this is a healthy change."

« « «   » » »

"Because of drinking, my friend Henry had lost a high-salaried job. There remained a fine house— with a budget three times his reduced earnings.

"He could have rented the house for enough to carry it. But no! Henry said he knew that God wanted him to live there, and He would see that the costs were paid. So Henry went on running up bills and glowing with faith. Not surprisingly, his creditors finally took over the place.

"Henry can laugh about it now, having learned that God more often helps those who are willing to help themselves."

1. LETTER, 1960
2. LETTER, 1966

Life Is Not a Dead End

When a man or a woman has a spiritual awakening, the most important meaning of it is that he has now become able to do, feel, and believe that which he could not do before on his unaided strength and resources alone. He has been granted a gift which amounts to a new state of consciousness and being.

He has been set on a path which tells him he is really going somewhere, that life is not a dead end, not something to be endured or mastered. In a very real sense he has been transformed, because he has laid hold of a source of strength which he had hitherto denied himself.

TWELVE AND TWELVE, PP. 106-107

Room for Improvement

We have come to believe that A.A.'s recovery Steps and Traditions represent the approximate truths which we need for our particular purpose. The more we practice them, the more we like them. So there is little doubt that A.A. principles will continue to be advocated in the form they stand now.

If our basics are so firmly fixed as all this, then what is there left to change or to improve?

The answer will immediately occur to us. While we need not alter our truths, we can surely improve their application to ourselves, to A.A. as a whole, and to our relation with the world around us. We can constantly step up the practice of "these principles in all our affairs."

GRAPEVINE, FEBRUARY 1961

Keystone of the Arch

Faced with alcoholic destruction, we became
open-minded on spiritual matters. In this respect
alcohol was a great persuader. It finally beat us
into a state of reasonableness.

«‹«   »›»

We had to quit playing God. It didn't work. We
decided that hereafter, in this drama of life, God
was going to be our Director. He would be the
Principal; we, His agents.

Most good ideas are simple, and this concept was
the keystone of the new triumphal arch through
which we passed to freedom.

ALCOHOLICS ANONYMOUS
1. P. 48
2. P. 62

Will Power and Choice

"We A.A.'s know the futility of trying to break the drinking obsession by will power alone. However, we do know that it takes great willingness to adopt A.A.'s Twelve Steps as a way of life that can restore us to sanity.

"No matter how grievous the alcohol obsession, we happily find that other vital choices can still be made. For example, we can choose to admit that we are personally powerless over alcohol; that dependence upon a 'Higher Power' is a necessity, even if this be simply dependence upon an A.A. group. Then we can choose to try for a life of honesty and humility, of selfless service to our fellows and to 'God as we understand Him.'

"As we continue to make these choices and so move toward these high aspirations, our sanity returns and the compulsion to drink vanishes."

LETTER, 1966

Review the Day

When we retire at night, we constructively review our day. Were we resentful, selfish, dishonest, or afraid? Do we owe an apology? Have we kept something to ourselves which should be discussed with another person at once? Were we kind and loving toward all? What could we have done better? Were we thinking of ourselves most of the time? Or were we thinking of what we could do for others, of what we could pack into the stream of life?

We must be careful not to drift into worry, remorse, or morbid reflection, for that would diminish our usefulness to ourselves and to others. After making our review, we ask God's forgiveness and inquire what corrective measures should be taken.

To Watch Loneliness Vanish

Almost without exception, alcoholics are tortured by loneliness. Even before our drinking got bad and people began to cut us off, nearly all of us suffered the feeling that we didn't quite belong. Either we were shy, and dared not draw near others, or we were noisy good fellows constantly craving attention and companionship, but rarely getting it. There was always that mysterious barrier we could neither surmount nor understand.

That's one reason we loved alcohol too well. But even Bacchus betrayed us; we were finally struck down and left in terrified isolation.

《《《   》》》

Life takes on new meaning in A.A. To watch people recover, to see them help others, to watch loneliness vanish, to see a fellowship grow up about you, to have a host of friends—this is an experience not to be missed.

1. TWELVE AND TWELVE, P. 57
2. ALCOHOLICS ANONYMOUS, P. 89

Courage and Prudence

When fear persisted, we knew it for what it was, and we became able to handle it. We began to see each adversity as a God-given opportunity to develop the kind of courage which is born of humility, rather than of bravado.

«««   »»»

Prudence is a workable middle ground, a channel of clear sailing between the obstacles of fear on the one side and of recklessness on the other. Prudence in practice creates a definite climate, the only climate in which harmony, effectiveness, and consistent spiritual progress can be achieved.

«««   »»»

"Prudence is rational concern without worry."

1. GRAPEVINE, JANUARY 1962
2. TWELVE CONCEPTS, P. 62
3. TALK, 1966

Walking Toward Serenity

"When I was tired and couldn't concentrate, I used to fall back on an affirmation toward life that took the form of simple walking and deep breathing. I sometimes told myself that I couldn't do even this—that I was too weak. But I learned that this was the point at which I could not give in without becoming still more depressed.

"So I would set myself a small stint. I would determine to walk a quarter of a mile. And I would concentrate by counting my breathing— say, six steps to each slow inhalation and four to each exhalation. Having done the quarter-mile, I found that I could go on, maybe a half-mile more. Then another half-mile, and maybe another.

"This was encouraging. The false sense of physical weakness would leave me (this feeling being so characteristic of depressions). The walking and especially the breathing were powerful affirmations toward life and living and away from failure and death. The counting represented a minimum discipline in concentration, to get some rest from the wear and tear of fear and guilt."

LETTER, 1960

93

Atmosphere of Grace

Those of us who have come to make regular use
of prayer would no more do without it than we
would refuse air, food, or sunshine. And for the
same reason. When we refuse air, light, or food,
the body suffers. And when we turn away from
meditation and prayer, we likewise deprive
our minds, our emotions, and our intuitions of
vitally needed support.

As the body can fail its purpose for lack of
nourishment, so can the soul. We all need the
light of God's reality, the nourishment of His
strength, and the atmosphere of His grace. To an
amazing extent the facts of A.A. life confirm this
ageless truth.

TWELVE AND TWELVE, PP. 97-98

". . . In All Our Affairs

"The chief purpose of A.A. is sobriety. We all realize that without sobriety we have nothing.

"However, it is possible to expand this simple aim into a great deal of nonsense, so far as the individual member is concerned. Sometimes we hear him say, in effect, 'Sobriety is my sole responsibility. After all, I'm a pretty fine chap, except for my drinking. Give me sobriety, and I've got it made!'

"As long as our friend clings to this comfortable alibi, he will make so little progress with his real life problems and responsibilities that he stands in a fair way to get drunk again. This is why A.A.'s Twelfth Step urges that we 'practice these principles in all our affairs.' We are not living just to be sober; we are living to learn, to serve, and to love."

LETTER, 1966

Spiritual Kindergarten

"We are only operating a spiritual kindergarten in
which people are enabled to get over drinking
and find the grace to go on living to better
effect. Each man's theology has to be his own
quest, his own affair."

≪ ≪ ≪　≫ ≫ ≫

When the Big Book was being planned, some
members thought that it ought to be Christian in
the doctrinal sense. Others had no objection to
the use of the word "God," but wanted to avoid
doctrinal issues. Spirituality, yes. Religion, no.
Still others wanted a psychological book, to lure
the alcoholic in. Once in, he could take God or
leave Him alone as he wished.

To the rest of us this was shocking, but happily
we listened. Our group conscience was at work to
construct the most acceptable and effective book
possible.

Every voice was playing its appointed part. Our
atheists and agnostics widened our gateway so
that all who suffer might pass through, regardless
of their belief or lack of belief.

1. LETTER, 1954
2. A.A. COMES OF AGE, PP. 162, 163, 167

When Defects Are Less than Deadly

Practically everybody wishes to be rid of his most glaring and destructive handicaps. No one wants to be so proud that he is scorned as a braggart, nor so greedy that he is labeled a thief. No one wants to be angry enough to murder, lustful enough to rape, gluttonous enough to ruin his health. No one wants to be agonized by chronic envy or paralyzed by sloth.

Of course, most human beings don't suffer these defects at these rock-bottom levels, and we who have escaped such extremes are apt to congratulate ourselves. Yet can we? After all, hasn't it been self-interest that has enabled most of us to escape? Not much spiritual effort is involved in avoiding excesses which will bring us punishment anyway. But when we face up to the less violent aspects of these very same defects, where do we stand then?

TWELVE AND TWELVE, P. 66

Self-Respect Through Sacrifice

At the beginning we sacrificed alcohol. We had to, or it would have killed us. But we couldn't get rid of alcohol unless we made other sacrifices. We had to toss self-justification, self-pity, and anger right out the window. We had to quit the crazy contest for personal prestige and big bank balances. We had to take personal responsibility for our sorry state and quit blaming others for it.

Were these sacrifices? Yes, they were. To gain enough humility and self-respect to stay alive at all, we had to give up what had really been our dearest possessions—our ambition and our illegitimate pride.

A.A. COMES OF AGE, P. 287

Anger—Personal and Group Enemy

"As the book 'Alcoholics Anonymous' puts it, 'Resentment is the Number One offender.' It is a primary cause of relapses into drinking. How well we of A.A. know that for us 'To drink is eventually to go mad or die.'

"Much the same penalty overhangs every A.A. group. Given enough anger, both unity and purpose are lost. Given still more 'righteous' indignation, the group can disintegrate; it can actually die. This is why we avoid controversy. This is why we prescribe no punishments for any misbehavior, no matter how grievous. Indeed, no alcoholic can be deprived of his membership for any reason whatever.

"Punishment never heals. Only love can heal."

LETTER, 1966

The "Slipper" Needs Understanding

"Slips can often be charged to rebellion; some of us are more rebellious than others. Slips may be due to the illusion that one can be 'cured' of alcoholism. Slips can also be charged to carelessness and complacency. Many of us fail to ride out these periods sober. Things go fine for two or three years—then the member is seen no more. Some of us suffer extreme guilt because of vices or practices that we can't or won't let go of. Too little self-forgiveness and too little prayer —well, this combination adds up to slips.

"Then some of us are far more alcohol-damaged than others. Still others encounter a series of calamities and cannot seem to find the spiritual resources to meet them. There are those of us who are physically ill. Others are subject to more or less continuous exhaustion, anxiety, and depression. These conditions often play a part in slips—sometimes they are utterly controlling."

TALK, 1960

The Forgotten Mountain

When I was a child, I acquired some of the traits that had a lot to do with my insatiable craving for alcohol. I was brought up in a little town in Vermont, under the shadow of Mount Aeolus. An early recollection is that of looking up at this vast and mysterious mountain, wondering what it meant and whether I could ever climb that high. But I was presently distracted by my aunt who, as a fourth-birthday present, made me a plate of fudge. For the next thirty-five years I pursued the fudge of life and quite forgot about the mountain.

«««   »»»

When self-indulgence is less than ruinous, we have a milder word for it. We call it "taking our comfort."

1. A.A. COMES OF AGE, PP. 52-53
2. TWELVE AND TWELVE, P. 67

"The Spiritual Angle"

How often do we sit in A.A. meetings and hear the speaker declare, "But I haven't yet got the spiritual angle." Prior to this statement, he has described a miracle of transformation which has occurred in him—not only his release from alcohol, but a complete change in his whole attitude toward life and the living of it.

It is apparent to everyone else present that he has received a great gift, and that this gift is all out of proportion to anything that may be expected from simple A.A. participation. So we in the audience smile and say to ourselves, "Well, that guy is just reeking with the spiritual angle—except that he doesn't seem to know it yet!"

Healing Talk

When we consult an A.A. friend, we should not be reluctant to remind him of our need for full privacy. Intimate communication is normally so free and easy among us that an A.A. adviser may sometimes forget when we expect him to remain silent. The protective sanctity of this most healing of human relations ought never be violated.

Such privileged communications have priceless advantages. We find in them the perfect opportunity to be as honest as we know how to be. We do not have to think of the possibility of damage to other people, nor need we fear ridicule or condemnation. Here, too, we have the best possible chance of spotting self-deception.

Principle Before Expediency

Most of us thought good character was desirable.
Obviously, good character was something one
needed to get on with the business of being self-
satisfied. With a proper display of honesty and
morality, we'd stand a better chance of getting
what we really wanted. But whenever we had to
choose between character and comfort, character-
building was lost in the dust of our chase
after what we thought was happiness.

Seldom did we look at character-building as something desirable in itself. We never thought of
making honesty, tolerance, and true love of man
and God the daily basis of living.

«« «   » »»

How to translate a right mental conviction into a
right emotional result, and so into easy, happy,
and good living, is the problem of life itself.

1. TWELVE AND TWELVE, PP. 71-72
2. GRAPEVINE, JANUARY 1958

104

Our New Employer

We had a new Employer. Being all powerful, He provided what we needed, if we kept close to Him and performed His work well.

Established on such a footing, we became less and less interested in ourselves, our little plans and designs. More and more we became interested in seeing what we could contribute to life.

As we felt new power flow in, as we enjoyed peace of mind, as we discovered we could face life successfully, as we became conscious of His presence, we began to lose our fear of today, tomorrow, or the hereafter. We were reborn.

Move Ahead

To spend too much time on any one alcoholic is
to deny some other an opportunity to live and be
happy. One of our Fellowship failed entirely with
his first half-dozen prospects. He often says
that if he had continued to work on them, he
might have deprived many others, who have since
recovered, of their chance.

«««   »»»

"Our chief responsibility to the newcomer is an
adequate presentation of the program. If he does
nothing or argues, we do nothing but maintain
our own sobriety. If he starts to move ahead, even
a little, with an open mind, we then break our
necks to help in every way we can."

1. ALCOHOLICS ANONYMOUS, P. 96
2. LETTER, 1942

"Perfect" Humility

For myself, I try to seek out the truest definition of humility that I can. This will not be the perfect definition, because I shall always be imperfect.

At this writing, I would choose one like this: "Absolute humility would consist of a state of complete freedom from myself, freedom from all the claims that my defects of character now lay so heavily upon me. Perfect humility would be a full willingness, in all times and places, to find and to do the will of God."

When I meditate upon such a vision, I need not be dismayed because I shall never attain it, nor need I swell with presumption that one of these days its virtues shall all be mine.

I only need to dwell on the vision itself, letting it grow and ever more fill my heart. This done, I can compare it with my last-taken personal inventory. Then I get a sane and healthy idea of where I stand on the highway to humility. I see that my journey toward God has scarce begun.

As I thus get down to my right size and stature, my self-concern and importance become amusing.

Two Kinds of Pride

The prideful righteousness of "good people" may often be just as destructive as the glaring sins of those who are supposedly not so good.

« « «   » » »

We loved to shout the damaging fact that millions of the "good men of religion" were still killing one another off in the name of God. This all meant, of course, that we had substituted negative for positive thinking.

After we came to A.A., we had to recognize that this trait had been an ego-feeding proposition. In belaboring the sins of some religious people, we could feel superior to all of them. Moreover, we could avoid looking at some of our own shortcomings.

Self-righteousness, the very thing that we had contemptuously condemned in others, was our own besetting evil. This phony form of respectability was our undoing, so far as faith was concerned. But finally, driven to A.A., we learned better.

1. GRAPEVINE, AUGUST 1961
2. TWELVE AND TWELVE, P. 30

Learn in Quiet

In 1941, a news clipping was called to our attention by a New York member. In an obituary notice from a local paper, there appeared these words: "God grant us the serenity to accept the things we cannot change, the courage to change the things we can, and the wisdom to know the difference."

Never had we seen so much A.A. in so few words. With amazing speed the Serenity Prayer came into general use.

««« »»»

In meditation, debate has no place. We rest quietly with the thoughts or prayers of spiritually centered people who understand, so that we may experience and learn. This is the state of being that so often discovers and deepens a conscious contact with God.

1. A.A. COMES OF AGE, P. 196
2. TWELVE AND TWELVE, PP. 100-101

Freedom Through Acceptance

We admitted we couldn't lick alcohol with our own remaining resources, and so we accepted the further fact that dependence upon a Higher Power (if only our A.A. group) could do this hitherto impossible job. The moment we were able to accept these facts fully, our release from the alcohol compulsion had begun.

For most of us, this pair of acceptances had required a lot of exertion to achieve. Our whole treasured philosophy of self-sufficiency had to be cast aside. This had not been done with sheer will power; it came instead as the result of developing the willingness to accept these new facts of living.

We neither ran nor fought. But accept we did. And then we began to be free.

GRAPEVINE, MARCH 1962

Trouble: Constructive or Destructive?

"There was a time when we ignored trouble, hoping it would go away. Or, in fear and in depression, we ran from it, but found it was still with us. Often, full of unreason, bitterness, and blame, we fought back. These mistaken attitudes, powered by alcohol, guaranteed our destruction, unless they were altered.

"Then came A.A. Here we learned that trouble was really a fact of life for everybody—a fact that had to be understood and dealt with. Surprisingly, we found that our troubles could, under God's grace, be converted into unimagined blessings.

"Indeed, that was the essence of A.A. itself: trouble accepted, trouble squarely faced with calm courage, trouble lessened and often transcended. This was the A.A. story, and we became a part of it. Such demonstrations became our stock in trade for the next sufferer."

LETTER, 1966

Surveying the Past

We should make an accurate and really exhaustive survey of our past life as it has affected other people. In many instances we shall find that, though the harm done others has not been great, we have nevertheless done ourselves considerable emotional injury.

Then, too, damaging emotional conflicts persist below the level of consciousness, very deep, sometimes quite forgotten. Therefore, we should try hard to recall and review those past events which originally induced these conflicts and which continue to give our emotions violent twists, thus discoloring our personalities and altering our lives for the worse.

«« « » »»

"We reacted more strongly to frustrations than normal people. By reliving these episodes and discussing them in strict confidence with somebody else, we can reduce their size and therefore their potency in the unconscious."

1. TWELVE AND TWELVE, PP. 79-80
2. LETTER, 1957

112

Complete Security?

Upon entering A.A., the spectacle of years of waste threw us into panic. Financial importance was no longer our principal aim; we now clamored for material security.

Even when we were re-established in our business, terrible fears often continued to haunt us. This made us misers and penny-pinchers all over again. Complete financial security we must have—or else.

We forgot that most alcoholics in A.A. have an earning power considerably above average; we forgot the immense good will of our brother A.A.'s who were only too eager to help us to better jobs when we deserved them; we forgot the actual or potential financial insecurity of every human being in the world. And, worst of all, we forgot God. In money matters we had faith only in ourselves, and not too much of that.

To Be Fair-Minded

Too often, I think, we have deprecated and even derided projects of our friends in the field of alcoholism just because we do not always see eye to eye with them.

We should very seriously ask ourselves how many alcoholics have gone on drinking simply because we have failed to cooperate in good spirit with these many agencies—whether they be good, bad, or indifferent. No alcoholic should go mad or die merely because he did not come straight to A.A. at the beginning.

« « «   » » »

Our first objective will be the development of self-restraint. This carries a top-priority rating. When we speak or act hastily or rashly, the ability to be fair-minded and tolerant evaporates on the spot.

1. GRAPEVINE, JULY 1965
2. TWELVE AND TWELVE, P. 91

114

No Personal Power

"At first, the remedy for my personal difficulties seemed so obvious that I could not imagine any alcoholic turning the proposition down were it properly presented to him. Believing so firmly that Christ can do anything, I had the unconscious conceit to suppose that He would do everything through me—right then and in the manner I chose. After six long months, I had to admit that not a soul had surely laid hold of the Master— not excepting myself.

"This brought me to the good healthy realization that there were plenty of situations left in the world over which I had no personal power—that if I was so ready to admit that to be the case with alcohol, so I must make the same admission with respect to much else. I would have to be still and know that He, not I, was God."

LETTER, 1940

Essence of Growth

Let us never fear needed change. Certainly we have to discriminate between changes for worse and changes for better. But once a need becomes clearly apparent in an individual, in a group, or in A.A. as a whole, it has long since been found out that we cannot stand still and look the other way.

The essence of all growth is a willingness to change for the better and then an unremitting willingness to shoulder whatever responsibility this entails.

Each Man's Vision

"Beyond a Higher Power, as each of us may
vision Him, A.A. must never, as a society, enter
the field of dogma or theology. We can never become a religion in that sense, lest we kill our usefulness by getting bogged down in theological
contention."

《《《　》》》

"The really amazing fact about A.A. is that all
religions see in our program a resemblance to
themselves. For example, Catholic theologians
declare our Twelve Steps to be in exact accord
with their Ignatian Exercises for Retreat, and,
though our book reeks of sin, sickness, and death,
the Christian Science Monitor has often praised it
editorially.

"Now, looking through Quaker eyes, you, too, see
us favorably. What happy circumstances, these!"

1. LETTER, 1954
2. LETTER, 1950

The Sense of Belonging

Perhaps one of the greatest rewards of meditation and prayer is the sense of belonging that comes to us. We no longer live in a completely hostile world. We are no longer lost and frightened and purposeless.

The moment we catch even a glimpse of God's will, the moment we begin to see truth, justice, and love as the real and eternal things in life, we are no longer deeply disturbed by all the seeming evidence to the contrary that surrounds us in purely human affairs. We know that God lovingly watches over us. We know that when we turn to Him, all will be well with us, here and hereafter.

Prelude to the Program

Few people will sincerely try to practice the A.A. program unless they have "hit bottom," for practicing A.A.'s Steps means the adoption of attitudes and actions that almost no alcoholic who is still drinking can dream of taking. The average alcoholic, self-centered in the extreme, doesn't care for this prospect—unless he has to do these things in order to stay alive himself.

«««   »»»

We know that the newcomer has to "hit bottom"; otherwise, not much can happen. Because we are drunks who understand him, we can use at depth the nutcracker of the-obsession-plus-the-allergy as a tool of such power that it can shatter his ego. Only thus can he be convinced that on his own unaided resources he has little or no chance.

1. TWELVE AND TWELVE, P. 24
2. A.A. TODAY, P. 8

On the Broad Highway

"I now realize that my former prejudice against clergymen was blind and wrong. They have kept alive through the centuries a faith which might have been extinguished entirely. They pointed out the road to me, but I did not even look up, I was so full of prejudice and self-concern.

"When I did open my eyes, it was because I had to. And the man who showed me the truth was a fellow sufferer and a layman. Through him, I saw at last, and I stepped from the abyss to solid ground, knowing at once that my feet were on the broad highway if I chose to walk."

LETTER, 1940

Word of Mouth

"In my view, there isn't the slightest objection to groups who wish to remain strictly anonymous, or to people who think they would not like their membership in A.A. known at all. That is their business, and this is a very natural reaction.

"However, most people find that anonymity to this degree is not necessary, or even desirable. Once one is fairly sober, and sure of this, there seems no reason for failing to talk about A.A. membership in the right places. This has a tendency to bring in other people. Word of mouth is one of our most important communications.

"So we should criticize neither the people who wish to remain silent, nor even the people who wish to talk too much about belonging to A.A., provided they do not do so at the public level and thus compromise our whole Society."

LETTER, 1962

We Are Not Fighting

We have ceased fighting anything or anyone—
even alcohol. For by this time sanity has returned.
We can now react sanely and normally, and we
find that this has happened almost automatically.
We see that this new attitude toward liquor
is really a gift of God.

That is the miracle of it. We are not fighting it,
neither are we avoiding temptation. We have not
even sworn off. Instead, the problem has been
removed. It does not exist for us. We
are neither cocky nor are we afraid.

That is how we react—so long as we keep in fit
spiritual condition.

Willingness Is the Key

No matter how much one wishes to try, exactly how can he turn his own will and his own life over to the care of whatever God he thinks there is?

A beginning, even the smallest, is all that is needed. Once we have placed the key of willingness in the lock and have the door ever so slightly open, we find that we can always open it some more.

Though self-will may slam it shut again, as it frequently does, it will always respond the moment we again pick up the key of willingness.

TWELVE AND TWELVE, P. 35

The New A.A. and His Family

When alcoholism strikes, very unnatural situations may develop which work against marriage partnership and compatible union. If the man is affected, the wife must become the head of the house, often the breadwinner. As matters get worse, the husband becomes a sick and irresponsible child who needs to be looked after and extricated from endless scrapes and impasses. Very gradually, usually without any realization of the fact, the wife is forced to become the mother of an erring boy, and the alcoholic alternately loves and hates her maternal care.

Under the influence of A.A.'s Twelve Steps, these situations are often set right.

《《《   》》》

Whether the family goes on a spiritual basis or not, the alcoholic member has to if he would recover. The others must be convinced of his new status beyond the shadow of a doubt. Seeing is believing to most families who have lived with a drinker.

1. TWELVE AND TWELVE, PP. 117-118
2. ALCOHOLICS ANONYMOUS, P. 135

Freedom to Choose

Looking back, we see that our freedom to choose badly was not, after all, a very real freedom.

When we chose because we "must," this was not a free choice, either. But it got us started in the right direction.

When we chose because we "ought to," we were really doing better. This time we were earning some freedom, making ourselves ready for more.

But when, now and then, we could gladly make right choices without rebellion, hold-out, or conflict, then we had our first view of what perfect freedom under God's will could be like.

GRAPEVINE, MAY 1960

Look Beyond the Horizon

My workshop stands on a hill back of our home.
Looking over the valley, I see the village
community house where our local group meets.
Beyond the circle of my horizon lies the
whole world of A.A.

«««   »»»

The unity of A.A. is the most cherished quality
our Society has. Our lives, the lives of all to come,
depend squarely upon it. Without unity, the heart
of A.A. would cease to beat; our world arteries
would no longer carry the life-giving grace
of God.

1. A.A. TODAY, P. 7
2. TWELVE AND TWELVE, P. 129

"Admitted to God . . . "

Provided you hold back nothing in taking the
Fifth Step, your sense of relief will mount from
minute to minute. The dammed-up emotions of
years break out of their confinement, and
miraculously vanish as soon as they are exposed.
As the pain subsides, a healing tranquillity takes
its place. And when humility and serenity are
so combined, something else of great moment is
apt to occur.

Many an A.A., once agnostic or atheist, tells us
that it was during this stage of Step Five that
he first actually felt the presence of God. And
even those who already had faith often
become conscious of God as they never were
before.

Persistence in Prayer

We often tend to slight serious meditation and
prayer as something not really necessary. To be
sure, we feel it is something that might help
us to meet an occasional emergency, but at first
many of us are apt to regard it as a somewhat
mysterious skill of clergymen, from which
we may hope to get a secondhand benefit.

In A.A. we have found that the actual good
results of prayer are beyond question. They are
matters of knowledge and experience. All
those who have persisted have found strength not
ordinarily their own. They have found wisdom
beyond their usual capability. And they have
increasingly found a peace of mind which can
stand firm in the face of difficult circumstances.

TWELVE AND TWELVE
1. p. 96
2. p. 104

Back to Work

It is possible for us to use the alleged dishonesty of other people as a plausible excuse for not meeting our own obligations.

Once, some prejudiced friends exhorted me never to go back to Wall Street. They were sure that the rampant materialism and double-dealing down there would stunt my spiritual growth. Because this sounded so high-minded, I continued to stay away from the only business that I knew.

When, finally, my household went broke, I realized I hadn't been able to face the prospect of going back to work. So I returned to Wall Street, and I have ever since been glad that I did. I needed to rediscover that there are many fine people in New York's financial district. Then, too, I needed the experience of staying sober in the very surroundings where alcohol had cut me down.

A Wall Street business trip to Akron, Ohio, first brought me face to face with Dr. Bob. So the birth of A.A. hinged on my effort to meet my bread-and-butter responsibilities.

GRAPEVINE, AUGUST 1961

129

The Way of Strength

We need not apologize to anyone for depending upon the Creator. We have good reason to disbelieve those who think spirituality is the way of weakness. For us, it is the way of strength.

The verdict of the ages is that men of faith seldom lack courage. They trust their God. So we never apologize for our belief in Him. Instead, we try to let Him demonstrate, through us, what He can do.

Our Problem Centers in the Mind

We know that as long as the alcoholic keeps away from drink, he usually reacts much like other men. We are equally positive that once he takes any alcohol whatever into his system, something happens, in both the bodily and the mental sense, which makes it virtually impossible for him to stop. The experience of any alcoholic will abundantly confirm this.

These observations would be academic and pointless if our friend never took the first drink, thereby setting the terrible cycle in motion. Therefore, the main problem of the alcoholic centers in his mind, rather than in his body.

Obstacles in Our Path

We live in a world riddled with envy. To a
greater or lesser degree, everybody is infected with
it. From this defect we must surely get a warped
yet definite satisfaction. Else why would we
consume so much time wishing for what we have
not, rather than working for it, or angrily looking
for attributes we shall never have, instead of
adjusting to the fact, and accepting it?

«« « » » »

Each of us would like to live at peace with himself and with his fellows. We would like to be
assured that the grace of God can do for us what
we cannot do for ourselves.

We have seen that character defects based upon
shortsighted or unworthy desires are the obstacles
that block our path toward these objectives. We
now clearly see that we have been making unreasonable demands upon ourselves, upon others,
and upon God.

TWELVE AND TWELVE
1. P. 67
2. P. 76

132

Spot-Checking

A spot-check inventory taken in the midst of disturbances can be of very great help in quieting stormy emotions. Today's spot check finds its chief application to situations which arise in each day's march. The consideration of long-standing difficulties had better be postponed, when possible, to times deliberately set aside for that purpose.

The quick inventory is aimed at our daily ups and downs, especially those where people or new events throw us off balance and tempt us to make mistakes.

"Privileged People"

I saw that I had been living too much alone, too much aloof from my fellows, and too deaf to that voice within. Instead of seeing myself as a simple agent bearing the message of experience, I had thought of myself as a founder of A.A.

How much better it would have been had I felt gratitude rather than self-satisfaction—gratitude that I had once suffered the pains of alcoholism, gratitude that a miracle of recovery had been worked upon me from above, gratitude for the privilege of serving my fellow alcoholics, and gratitude for those fraternal ties which bound me ever closer to them in a comradeship such as few societies of men have ever known.

Truly did a clergyman say to me, "Your misfortune has become your good fortune. You A.A.'s are a privileged people."

The Individual's Rights

We believe there isn't a fellowship on earth which devotes more care to its individual members; surely there is none which more jealously guards the individual's right to think, talk, and act as he wishes. No A.A. can compel another to do anything; nobody can be punished or expelled.

Our Twelve Steps to recovery are suggestions; the Twelve Traditions which guarantee A.A.'s unity contain not a single "Don't." They repeatedly say, "We ought . . ." but never "You must!"

《《《   》》》

"Though it is traditional that our Fellowship may not coerce anyone, let us not suppose even for an instant that we are not under constraint. Indeed, we are under enormous coercion—the kind that comes in bottles. Our former tyrant, King Alcohol, always stands ready again to clutch us to him.

"Therefore, freedom from alcohol is the great 'must' that has to be achieved, else we go mad or die."

1. TWELVE AND TWELVE, P. 129
2. LETTER, 1966

Victory in Defeat

Convinced I never could belong, and vowing I'd never settle for any second-rate status, I felt I simply had to dominate in everything I chose to do: work or play. As this attractive formula for the good life began to succeed, according to my then specifications of success, I became deliriously happy.

But when an undertaking occasionally did fail, I was filled with resentment and depression that could be cured only by the next triumph. Very early, therefore, I came to value everything in terms of victory or defeat—"all or nothing." The only satisfaction I knew was to win.

«« « » »»

Only through utter defeat are we able to take our first steps toward liberation and strength. Our admissions of personal powerlessness finally turn out to be firm bedrock upon which happy and purposeful lives may be built.

1. GRAPEVINE, JANUARY 1962
2. TWELVE AND TWELVE, P. 21

136

Giving Up Defects

Looking at those defects we are unwilling to give up, we ought to erase the hard and fast lines that we have drawn. Perhaps in some cases we shall say, "This I cannot give up yet. . . ." But we should not say to ourselves, "This I will never give up!"

The moment we say, "No, never!" our minds close against the grace of God. Such rebellion may be fatal. Instead, we should abandon limited objectives and begin to move toward God's will for us.

TWELVE AND TWELVE, PP. 68-69

Beyond Agnosticism

We of agnostic temperament found that as soon as we were able to lay aside prejudice and express even a willingness to believe in a Power greater than ourselves, we commenced to get results, even though it was impossible for any of us to fully define or comprehend that Power, which is God.

«« «   » »»

"Many people soberly assure me that man has no better place in the universe than that of another competing organism, fighting its way through life only to perish in the end. Hearing this, I feel that I still prefer to cling to the so-called illusion of religion, which in my own experience has meaningfully told me something very different."

1. ALCOHOLICS ANONYMOUS, P. 46
2. LETTER, 1946

Two Roads for the Oldtimer

The founders of many groups ultimately divide into two classes known in A.A. slang as "elder statesmen" and "bleeding deacons."

The elder statesman sees the wisdom of the group's decision to run itself and holds no resentment over his reduced status. His judgment, fortified by considerable experience, is sound; he is willing to sit quietly on the side lines patiently awaiting developments.

The bleeding deacon is just as surely convinced that the group cannot get along without him. He constantly connives for re-election to office and continues to be consumed with self-pity. Nearly every oldtimer in our Society has gone through this process in some degree. Happily, most of them survive and live to become elder statesmen. They become the real and permanent leadership of A.A.

Basis of All Humility

For just so long as we were convinced that we could live exclusively by our own individual strength and intelligence, for just that long was a working faith in a Higher Power impossible.

This was true even when we believed that God existed. We could actually have earnest religious beliefs which remained barren because we were still trying to play God ourselves. As long as we placed self-reliance first, a genuine reliance upon a Higher Power was out of the question.

That basic ingredient of all humility, a desire to seek and do God's will, was missing.

Defects and Repairs

More than most people, the alcoholic leads a double life. He is very much the actor. To the outer world he presents his stage character. This is the one he likes his fellows to see. He wants to enjoy a certain reputation, but knows in his heart he doesn't deserve it.

«« »»

Guilt is really the reverse side of the coin of pride. Guilt aims at self-destruction, and pride aims at the destruction of others.

«« »»

"The moral inventory is a cool examination of the damages that occurred to us during life and a sincere effort to look at them in a true perspective. This has the effect of taking the ground glass out of us, the emotional substance that still cuts and inhibits."

1. ALCOHOLICS ANONYMOUS, P. 73
2. GRAPEVINE, JUNE 1961
3. LETTER, 1957

"Restore Us to Sanity"

Few indeed are the practicing alcoholics who have any idea how irrational they are, or, seeing their irrationality, can bear to face it. For example, some will be willing to term themselves "problem drinkers," but cannot endure the suggestion that they are in fact mentally ill.

They are abetted in this blindness by a world which does not understand the difference between sane drinking and alcoholism. "Sanity" is defined as "soundness of mind." Yet no alcoholic, soberly analyzing his destructive behavior, whether the destruction fell on the dining-room furniture or his own moral fiber, can claim "soundness of mind" for himself.

TWELVE AND TWELVE, PP. 32-33

God-Given Instincts

Creation gave us instincts for a purpose. Without them we wouldn't be complete human beings. If men and women didn't exert themselves to be secure in their persons, made no effort to harvest food or construct shelter, there would be no survival. If they didn't reproduce, the earth wouldn't be populated. If there were no social instinct, there would be no society.

Yet these instincts, so necessary for our existence, often far exceed their proper functions. Powerfully, blindly, many times subtly, they drive us, dominate us, and insist upon ruling our lives.

«« »»

We tried to shape a sane ideal for our future sex life. We subjected each relation to this test: Was it selfish or not? We asked God to mold our ideals and help us to live up to them. We remembered always that our sex powers were God-given and therefore good, neither to be used lightly or selfishly nor to be despised and loathed.

1. TWELVE AND TWELVE, P. 42
2. ALCOHOLICS ANONYMOUS, P. 69

143

A.A.'s School of Life

Within A.A., I suppose, we shall always quarrel a good bit. Mostly, I think, about how to do the greatest good for the greatest number of drunks. We shall have our childish spats and snits over small questions of money management and who is going to run our groups for the next six months. Any bunch of growing children (and that is what we are) would hardly be in character if they did less.

These are the growing pains of infancy, and we actually thrive on them. Surmounting such problems, in A.A.'s rather rugged school of life, is a healthy exercise.

A.A. COMES OF AGE, P. 233

Blind Trust?

"Most surely, there can be no trust where there is no love, nor can there be real love where distrust holds its malign sway.

"But does trust require that we be blind to other people's motives or, indeed, to our own? Not at all; this would be folly. Most certainly, we should assess the capacity for harm as well as the capability for good in every person that we would trust. Such a private inventory can reveal the degree of confidence we should extend in any given situation.

"However, this inventory needs to be taken in a spirit of understanding and love. Nothing can so much bias our judgment as the negative emotions of suspicion, jealousy, or anger.

"Having vested our confidence in another person, we ought to let him know of our full support. Because of this, more often than not he will respond magnificently, and far beyond our first expectations."

LETTER, 1966

To Take Responsibility

Learning how to live in the greatest peace, partnership, and brotherhood with all men and women, of whatever description, is a moving and fascinating adventure.

But every A.A. has found that he can make little headway in this new adventure of living until he first backtracks and really makes an accurate and unsparing survey of the human wreckage he has left in his wake.

≪ ≪ ≪   ≫ ≫ ≫

The readiness to take the full consequences of our past acts, and to take responsibility for the well-being of others at the same time, is the very spirit of Step Nine.

TWELVE AND TWELVE
1. P. 77
2. P. 87

"Do as I Do . . ."

Perhaps more often than we think, we make no contact at depth with alcoholics who are suffering the dilemma of no faith.

Certainly none are more sensitive to spiritual cocksureness, pride, and aggression than they are. I'm sure this is something we too often forget.

In A.A.'s first years, I all but ruined the whole undertaking with this sort of unconscious arrogance. God as I understood Him had to be for everybody. Sometimes my aggression was subtle and sometimes it was crude. But either way it was damaging—perhaps fatally so—to numbers of nonbelievers.

Of course this sort of thing isn't confined to Twelfth Step work. It is very apt to leak out into our relations with everybody. Even now, I catch myself chanting that same old barrier-building refrain: "Do as I do, believe as I do—or else!"

A.A.—the Lodestar

We can be grateful for every agency or method that tries to solve the problem of alcoholism—whether of medicine, religion, education, or research. We can be open-minded toward all such efforts and we can be sympathetic when the ill-advised ones fail. We can remember that A.A. itself ran for years on "trial and error."

As individuals, we can and should work with those that promise success—even a little success.

« « «   » » »

Every one of the pioneers in the total field of alcoholism will generously say that had it not been for the living proof of recovery in A.A., they could not have gone on. A.A. was the lodestar of hope and help that kept them at it.

More than Comfort

When I am feeling depressed, I repeat to myself statements such as these: "Pain is the touchstone of progress." . . . "Fear no evil." . . . "This, too, will pass." . . . "This experience can be turned to benefit."

These fragments of prayer bring far more than mere comfort. They keep me on the track of right acceptance; they break up my compulsive themes of guilt, depression, rebellion, and pride; and sometimes they endow me with the courage to change the things I can, and the wisdom to know the difference.

Guide to a Better Way

Almost none of us liked the self-searching, the leveling of our pride, the confession of short-comings which the Steps require. But we saw that the program really worked in others, and we had come to believe in the hopelessness of life as we had been living it.

When, therefore, we were approached by those in whom the problem had been solved, there was nothing left for us but to pick up the simple kit of spiritual tools laid at our feet.

《《《　》》》

Implicit throughout A.A.'s Traditions is the confession that our Fellowship has its sins. We admit that we have character defects as a society and that these defects threaten us continually. Our Traditions are a guide to better ways of working and living, and they are to group survival and harmony what A.A.'s Twelve Steps are to each member's sobriety and peace of mind.

1. ALCOHOLICS ANONYMOUS, P. 25
2. A.A. COMES OF AGE, P. 96

150

No Boundaries

Meditation is something which can always be further developed. It has no boundaries, of width or height or depth. Aided by such instruction and example as we can find, it is essentially an individual adventure, something which each one of us works out in his own way. But its object is always the same: to improve our conscious contact with God, with His grace, wisdom, and love.

And let's always remember that meditation is in reality intensely practical. One of its first fruits is emotional balance. With it we can broaden and deepen the channel between ourselves and God as we understand Him.

TWELVE AND TWELVE, PP. 101-102

151

Start by Forgiving

The moment we ponder a twisted or broken relationship with another person, our emotions go on the defensive. To escape looking at the wrongs we have done another, we resentfully focus on the wrong he has done us. Triumphantly we seize upon his slightest misbehavior as the perfect excuse for minimizing or forgetting our own.

Right here we need to fetch ourselves up sharply. Let's remember that alcoholics are not the only ones bedeviled by sick emotions. In many instances we are really dealing with fellow sufferers, people whose woes we have increased.

If we are about to ask forgiveness for ourselves, why shouldn't we start out by forgiving them, one and all?

TWELVE AND TWELVE, P. 78

Miraculous Power

Deep down in every man, woman, and child is
the fundamental idea of a God. It may be ob-
scured by calamity, by pomp, by worship of
other things, but in some form or other it is there.
For faith in a Power greater than ourselves, and
miraculous demonstrations of that Power in human
lives are facts as old as man himself.

«««   »»»

"Faith may often be given through inspired teaching or a convincing personal example of its fruits.
It may sometimes be had through reason. For
instance, many clergymen believe that St. Thomas
Aquinas actually proved God's existence by sheer
logic. But what can one do when all these
channels fail? This was my own grievous dilemma.

"It was only when I came fully to believe I was
powerless over alcohol, only when I appealed to
a God who just might exist, that I experienced a
spiritual awakening. This freedom-giving experience came first, and then faith followed afterward
—a gift indeed!"

1. ALCOHOLICS ANONYMOUS, P. 55
2. LETTER, 1966

Without Anger

Suppose A.A. falls under sharp public attack or heavy ridicule, having little or no justification in fact. Our best defense in these situations would be no defense whatever—namely, complete silence at the public level. If in good humor we let unreasonable critics alone, they are apt to subside the more quickly. If their attacks persist and it is plain that they are misinformed, it may be wise to communicate with them privately in a temperate and informative way.

If, however, a given criticism of A.A. is partly or wholly justified, it may be well to acknowledge this privately to the critics, together with our thanks.

But under no conditions should we exhibit anger or any punitive intent.

《 《 《   》 》 》

What we must recognize is that we exult in some of our defects. Self-righteous anger can be very enjoyable. In a perverse way we can actually take satisfaction from the fact that many people annoy us; it brings a comfortable feeling of superiority.

1. TWELVE CONCEPTS, P. 69
2. TWELVE AND TWELVE, PP. 66–67

Relapses—and the Group

An early fear was that of slips or relapses. At first nearly every alcoholic we approached began to slip, if indeed he sobered up at all. Others would stay dry six months or maybe a year and then take a skid. This was always a genuine catastrophe. We would all look at each other and say, "Who next?"

Today, though slips are a very serious difficulty, as a group we take them in stride. Fear has evaporated. Alcohol always threatens the individual, but we know that it cannot destroy the common welfare.

« « «   » » »

"It does not seem to pay to argue with 'slippers' about the proper method of getting dry. After all, why should people who are drinking tell people who are dry how it should be done?

"Just kid the boys along—ask them if they are having fun. If they are too noisy or troublesome, amiably keep out of their way."

1. A.A. COMES OF AGE, P. 97
2. LETTER, 1942

Built by the One and the Many

We give thanks to our Heavenly Father, who, through so many friends and through so many means and channels, has allowed us to construct this wonderful edifice of the spirit in which we are now dwelling—this cathedral whose foundations already rest upon the corners of the earth.

On its great floor we have inscribed our Twelve Steps of recovery. On the side walls, the buttresses of the A.A. Traditions have been set in place to contain us in unity for as long as God may will it so. Eager hearts and hands have lifted the spire of our cathedral into its place. That spire bears the name of Service. May it ever point straight upward toward God.

《《《　》》》

"It is not only to the few that we owe the remarkable developments in our unity and in our ability to carry A.A.'s message everywhere. It is to the many; indeed, it is to the labors of all of us that we owe these prime blessings."

1. A.A. COMES OF AGE, P. 234
2. TALK, 1959

Perception of Humility

An improved perception of humility starts a
revolutionary change in our outlook. Our eyes
begin to open to the immense values which have
come straight out of painful ego-puncturing. Until
now, our lives have been largely devoted to
running from pain and problems. Escape via the
bottle was always our solution.

Then, in A.A., we looked and listened. Everywhere we saw failure and misery transformed by
humility into priceless assets.

《 《 《   》 》 》

To those who have made progress in A.A.,
humility amounts to a clear recognition of what
and who we really are, followed by a sincere
attempt to become what we could be.

TWELVE AND TWELVE
1. PP. 74-75
2. P. 58

Imagination Can Be Constructive

We recall, a little ruefully, how much store we used to set by imagination as it tried to create reality out of bottles. Yes, we reveled in that sort of thinking, didn't we? And, though sober nowadays, don't we often try to do much the same thing?

Perhaps our trouble was not that we used our imagination. Perhaps the real trouble was our almost total inability to point imagination toward the right objectives. There's nothing the matter with truly constructive imagination; all sound achievement rests upon it. After all, no man can build a house until he first visions a plan for it.

158

Tolerance in Practice

"We found that the principles of tolerance and love had to be emphasized in actual practice. We can never say (or insinuate) to anyone that he must agree to our formula or be excommunicated. The atheist may stand up in an A.A. meeting still denying the Deity, yet reporting how vastly he has been changed in attitude and outlook. Much experience tells us he will presently change his mind about God, but nobody tells him he must do so.

"In order to carry the principle of inclusiveness and tolerance still further, we make no religious requirement of anyone. All people having an alcoholic problem who wish to get rid of it and so make a happy adjustment with the circumstances of their lives, become A.A. members by simply associating with us. Nothing but sincerity is needed. But we do not demand even this.

"In such an atmosphere the orthodox, the unorthodox, and the unbeliever mix happily and usefully together. An opportunity for spiritual growth is open to all."

LETTER, 1940

Between the Extremes

"The real question is whether we can learn anything from our experiences upon which we may grow and help others to grow in the likeness and image of God.

"We know that if we rebel against doing that which is reasonably possible for us, then we will be penalized. And we will be equally penalized if we presume in ourselves a perfection that simply is not there.

"Apparently, the course of relative humility and progress will have to lie somewhere between these extremes. In our slow progress away from rebellion, true perfection is doubtless several millennia away."

The Rationalizers and the Self-Effacing

We alcoholics are the biggest rationalizers in the world. Fortified with the excuse that we are doing great things for A.A., we can, through broken anonymity, resume our old and disastrous pursuit of personal power and prestige, public honors, and money—the same implacable urges that, when frustrated, once caused us to drink.

« « «   » » »

Dr. Bob was essentially a far more humble person than I, and anonymity came rather easily to him. When it was sure that he was mortally afflicted, some of his friends suggested that there should be a monument erected in honor of him and his wife, Anne—befitting a founder and his lady. Telling me about this, Dr. Bob grinned broadly and said, "God bless 'em. They mean well. But let's you and me get buried just like other folks."

In the Akron cemetery where Dr. Bob and Anne lie, the simple stone says not a word about A.A. This final example of self-effacement is of more permanent worth to A.A. than any amount of public attention or any great monument.

A.A. COMES OF AGE
1. PP. 292-293
2. PP. 136-137

Whose Inventory?

We do not relate intimate experiences of another
member unless we are sure he would approve. We
find it better, when possible, to stick to our own
stories. A man may criticize or laugh at himself
and it will affect others favorably, but criticism or
ridicule aimed at someone else often produces the
contrary effect.

《《《　》》》

A continuous look at our assets and liabilities,
and a real desire to learn and grow by this means
are necessities for us. We alcoholics have learned
this the hard way. More experienced people, of
course, in all times and places have practiced
unsparing self-survey and criticism.

1. ALCOHOLICS ANONYMOUS, P. 125
2. TWELVE AND TWELVE, P. 88

162

"Let's Keep It Simple"

"We need to distinguish sharply between spiritual simplicity and functional simplicity.

"When we say that A.A. advocates no theological proposition except God as we understand Him, we greatly simplify A.A. life by avoiding conflict and exclusiveness.

"But when we get into questions of action by groups, by areas, and by A.A. as a whole, we find that we must to some extent organize to carry the message—or else face chaos. And chaos is not simplicity."

« « «   » » »

I learned that the temporary or seeming good can often be the deadly enemy of the permanent best. When it comes to survival for A.A., nothing short of our very best will be good enough.

1. LETTER, 1966
2. A.A. COMES OF AGE, P. 294

Release and Joy

Who can render an account of all the miseries
that once were ours, and who can estimate the
release and joy that the later years have brought
to us? Who can possibly tell the vast consequences
of what God's work through A.A. has already set
in motion?

And who can penetrate the deeper mystery of our
wholesale deliverance from slavery, a bondage to
a most hopeless and fatal obsession which for
centuries possessed the minds and bodies of men
and women like ourselves?

«««   »»»

We think cheerfulness and laughter make for
usefulness. Outsiders are sometimes shocked when
we burst into merriment over a seemingly tragic
experience out of the past. But why shouldn't we
laugh? We have recovered, and have helped others
to recover. What greater cause could there be for
rejoicing than this?

1. A.A. COMES OF AGE, PP. 44-45
2. ALCOHOLICS ANONYMOUS, P. 132

A Saving Principle

The practice of admitting one's defects to another person is, of course, very ancient. It has been validated in every century, and it characterizes the lives of all spiritually centered and truly religious people.

But today religion is by no means the sole advocate of this saving principle. Psychiatrists and psychologists point out the deep need every human being has for practical insight and knowledge of his own personality flaws and for a discussion of them with an understanding and trustworthy person.

So far as alcoholics are concerned, A.A. would go even further. Most of us would declare that without a fearless admission of our defects to another human being, we could not stay sober. It seems plain that the grace of God will not enter to expel our destructive obsessions until we are willing to try this.

TWELVE AND TWELVE, PP. 56-57

"Success" in Twelfth-Stepping

"We now see that in twelfth-stepping the immediate results are not so important. Some people start out working with others and have immediate success. They are likely to get cocky. Those of us who are not so successful at first get depressed.

"As a matter of fact, the successful worker differs from the unsuccessful only in being lucky about his prospects. He simply hits newcomers who are ready and able to stop at once. Given the same prospects, the seemingly unsuccessful person would have produced almost the same results. You have to work on a lot of newcomers before the law of averages commences to assert itself."

《 《 《   》 》 》

All true communication must be founded on mutual need. We saw that each sponsor would have to admit humbly his own needs as clearly as those of his prospect.

1. LETTER, 1942
2. A.A. TODAY, P. 10

Fear No Evil

Though we of A.A. find ourselves living in a world characterized by destructive fears as never before in history, we see great areas of faith, and tremendous aspirations toward justice and brotherhood. Yet no prophet can presume to say whether the world outcome will be blazing destruction or the beginning, under God's intention, of the brightest era yet known to mankind.

I am sure we A.A.'s will comprehend this scene. In microcosm, we have experienced this identical state of terrifying uncertainty, each in his own life. In no sense pridefully, we can say that we do not fear the world outcome, whichever course it may take. This is because we have been enabled to deeply feel and say, "We shall fear no evil— Thy will, not ours, be done."

Progress Rather than Perfection

On studying the Twelve Steps, many of us exclaimed, "What an order! I can't go through with it." Do not be discouraged. No one among us has been able to maintain anything like perfect adherence to these principles. We are not saints.

The point is that we are willing to grow along spiritual lines. The principles we have set down are guides to progress. We claim spiritual progress rather than spiritual perfection.

«« «   » »»

"We recovered alcoholics are not so much brothers in virtue as we are brothers in our defects, and in our common strivings to overcome them."

1. ALCOHOLICS ANONYMOUS, P. 60
2. LETTER, 1946

Accepting God's Gifts

"Though many theologians hold that sudden spiritual experiences amount to a special distinction, if not a divine appointment of some sort, I question this view. Every human being, no matter what his attributes for good or evil, is a part of the divine spiritual economy. Therefore, each of us has his place, and I cannot see that God intends to exalt one over another.

"So it is necessary for all of us to accept whatever positive gifts we receive with a deep humility, always bearing in mind that our negative attitudes were first necessary as a means of reducing us to such a state that we would be ready for a gift of the positive ones via the conversion experience. Your own alcoholism and the immense deflation that finally resulted are indeed the foundation upon which your spiritual experience rests."

LETTER, 1964

Learning Never Ends

"My experience as an oldtimer has to some degree paralleled your own and that of many others. We all find that the time comes when we are not allowed to manage and conduct the functional affairs of groups, areas, or, in my case, A.A. as a whole. In the end we can only be worth as much as our spiritual example has justified. To that extent, we become useful symbols—and that's just about it."

«« «   » »»

"I have become a pupil of the A.A. movement rather than the teacher I once thought I was."

1. LETTER, 1964
2. LETTER, 1949

Whose Will?

We have seen A.A.'s ask with much earnestness and faith for God's explicit guidance on matters ranging all the way from a shattering domestic or financial crisis to a minor personal fault, like tardiness. A man who tries to run his life rigidly by this kind of prayer, by this self-serving demand of God for replies, is a particularly disconcerting individual. To any questioning or criticism of his actions, he instantly proffers his reliance upon prayer for guidance in all matters great or small.

He may have forgotten the possibility that his own wishful thinking and the human tendency to rationalize have distorted his so-called guidance. With the best of intentions, he tends to force his will into all sorts of situations and problems with the comfortable assurance that he is acting under God's specific direction.

TWELVE AND TWELVE, PP. 103-104

Dividends and Mysteries

"The A.A. preoccupation with sobriety is sometimes misunderstood. To some, this single virtue appears to be the sole dividend of our Fellowship. We are thought to be dried-up drunks who otherwise have changed little, or not at all, for the better. Such a surmise widely misses the truth. We know that permanent sobriety can be attained only by a most revolutionary change in the life and outlook of the individual—by a spiritual awakening that can banish the desire to drink."

«« » »

"You are asking yourself, as all of us must: 'Who am I?' . . . 'Where am I?' . . . 'Whence do I go?' The process of enlightenment is usually slow. But, in the end, our seeking always brings a finding. These great mysteries are, after all, enshrined in complete simplicity. The willingness to grow is the essence of all spiritual development."

1. LETTER, 1966
2. LETTER, 1955

This Matter of Honesty

"Only God can fully know what absolute honesty is. Therefore, each of us has to conceive what this great ideal may be—to the best of our ability.

"Fallible as we all are, and will be in this life, it would be presumption to suppose that we could ever really achieve absolute honesty. The best we can do is to strive for a better quality of honesty.

"Sometimes we need to place love ahead of indiscriminate 'factual honesty.' We cannot, under the guise of 'perfect honesty,' cruelly and unnecessarily hurt others. Always one must ask, 'What is the best and most loving thing I can do?' "

LETTER, 1966

Roots of Reality

We started upon a personal inventory, Step Four. A business which takes no regular inventory usually goes broke. Taking a commercial inventory is a fact-finding and a fact-facing process. It is an effort to discover the truth about the stock in trade. One object is to disclose damaged or unsalable goods, to get rid of them promptly and without regret. If the owner of the business is to be successful, he cannot fool himself about values.

We had to do exactly the same thing with our lives. We had to take stock honestly.

《《《　 》》》

"Moments of perception can build into a lifetime of spiritual serenity, as I have excellent reason to know. Roots of reality, supplanting the neurotic underbrush, will hold fast despite the high winds of the forces which would destroy us, or which we would use to destroy ourselves."

1. ALCOHOLICS ANONYMOUS, P. 64
2. LETTER, 1949

Constructive Forces

Mine was exactly the kind of deep-seated block we so often see today in new people who say they are atheistic or agnostic. Their will to disbelieve is so powerful that apparently they prefer a date with the undertaker to an open-minded and experimental quest for God.

Happily for me, and for most of my kind who have since come along in A.A., the constructive forces brought to bear in our Fellowship have nearly always overcome this colossal obstinacy. Beaten into complete defeat by alcohol, confronted by the living proof of release, and surrounded by those who can speak to us from the heart, we have finally surrendered.

And then, paradoxically, we have found ourselves in a new dimension, the real world of spirit and faith. Enough willingness, enough open-mindedness —and there it is!

A.A. TODAY, P. 9

Aspects of Tolerance

All kinds of people have found their way into
A.A. Not too long ago, I sat talking in my office
with a member who bears the title of Countess.
That same night, I went to an A.A. meeting. It
was winter, and there was a mild-looking little
gent taking the coats. I said, "Who's that?"

And somebody answered, "Oh, he's been around
for a long time. Everybody likes him. He used to
be one of Al Capone's mob." That's how universal
A.A. is today.

《《《　　》》》

We have no desire to convince anyone that there
is only one way by which faith can be acquired.
All of us, whatever our race, creed, or color, are
the children of a living Creator, with whom we
may form a relationship upon simple and under-
standable terms as soon as we are willing and
honest enough to try.

1. A.A. COMES OF AGE, P. 102
2. ALCOHOLICS ANONYMOUS, P. 28

Domination and Demand

The primary fact that we fail to recognize is our total inability to form a true partnership with another human being. Our egomania digs two disastrous pitfalls. Either we insist upon dominating the people we know, or we depend upon them far too much.

If we lean too heavily on people, they will sooner or later fail us, for they are human, too, and cannot possibly meet our incessant demands. In this way our insecurity grows and festers.

When we habitually try to manipulate others to our own willful desires, they revolt, and resist us heavily. Then we develop hurt feelings, a sense of persecution, and a desire to retaliate.

« « «   » » »

My dependency meant demand—a demand for the possession and control of the people and the conditions surrounding me.

1. TWELVE AND TWELVE, P. 53
2. GRAPEVINE, JANUARY 1958

Money—Before and After

In our drinking time, we acted as if the money supply were inexhaustible, though between binges we'd sometimes go to the other extreme and become miserly. Without realizing it, we were just accumulating funds for the next spree. Money was the symbol of pleasure and self-importance. As our drinking became worse, money was only an urgent requirement which could supply us with the next drink and the temporary comfort of oblivion it brought.

« « «   » » »

Although financial recovery is on the way for many of us, we find we cannot place money first. For us, material well-being always follows spiritual progress; it never precedes.

1. TWELVE AND TWELVE, P. 120
2. ALCOHOLICS ANONYMOUS, P. 127

Down to Earth

Those of us who have spent much time in the world of spiritual make-believe have eventually seen the childishness of it. This dream world has been replaced by a great sense of purpose, accompanied by a growing consciousness of the power of God in our lives.

We have come to believe He would like us to keep our heads in the clouds with Him, but that our feet ought to be firmly planted on earth. That is where our fellow travelers are, and that is where our work must be done. These are the realities for us. We have found nothing incompatible between a powerful spiritual experience and a life of sane and happy usefulness.

Coping with Anger

Few people have been more victimized by resentments than have we alcoholics. A burst of temper could spoil a day, and a well-nursed grudge could make us miserably ineffective. Nor were we ever skillful in separating justified from unjustified anger. As we saw it, our wrath was always justified. Anger, that occasional luxury of more balanced people, could keep us on an emotional jag indefinitely. These "dry benders" often led straight to the bottle.

Nothing pays off like restraint of tongue and pen. We must avoid quick-tempered criticism, furious power-driven argument, sulking, and silent scorn. These are emotional booby traps baited with pride and vengefulness. When we are tempted by the bait, we should train ourselves to step back and think. We can neither think nor act to good purpose until the habit of self-restraint has become automatic.

TWELVE AND TWELVE
1. P. 90
2. P. 91

Community Problem

The answer to the problem of alcoholism seems to be in education—education in schoolrooms, in medical colleges, among clergymen and employers, in families, and in the public at large. From cradle to grave, the drunk and the potential alcoholic will have to be completely surrounded by a true and deep understanding and by a continuous barrage of information.

This means factual education, properly presented. Heretofore, much of this education has attacked the immorality of drinking rather than the illness of alcoholism.

Now who is going to do all this education? Obviously, it is both a community job and a job for specialists. Individually, we A.A.'s can help, but A.A. as such cannot, and should not, get directly into this field. Therefore, we must rely on other agencies, on outside friends and their willingness to supply great amounts of money and effort.

Imaginary Perfection

When we early A.A.'s got our first glimmer of how spiritually prideful we could be, we coined this expression: "Don't try to be a saint by Thursday!"

That oldtime admonition may look like another of those handy alibis that can excuse us from trying for our best. Yet a closer view reveals just the contrary. This is our A.A. way of warning against pride-blindness, and the imaginary perfections that we do not possess.

«« »»

Only Step One, where we made the 100 per cent admission that we were powerless over alcohol, can be practiced with absolute perfection. The remaining eleven Steps state perfect ideals. They are goals toward which we look, and the measuring sticks by which we estimate our progress.

1. GRAPEVINE, JUNE 1961
2. TWELVE AND TWELVE, P. 68

182

The Reality of Spiritual Experiences

"Perhaps you raise the question of hallucination versus the divine imagery of a genuine spiritual experience. I doubt if anyone has authoritatively defined what an hallucination really is. However, it is certain that all recipients of spiritual experiences declare for their reality. The best evidence of that reality is in the subsequent fruits. Those who receive these gifts of grace are very much changed people, almost invariably for the better. This can scarcely be said of those who hallucinate.

"Some might think me presumptuous when I say that my own experience is real. Nevertheless, I can surely report that in my own life and in the lives of countless others, the fruits of that experience have been real, and the benefactions beyond reckoning."

A Viewer-with-Alarm

"I went through several fruitless years in a state called 'viewing with alarm for the good of the movement.' I thought it was up to me to be always 'correcting conditions.' Seldom had anybody been able to tell me what I ought to do, and nobody had ever succeeded in effectively telling me what I must do. I had to learn the hard way out of my own experience.

"When setting out to 'check' others, I found myself often motivated by fear of what they were doing, self-righteousness, and even downright intolerance. Consequently, I seldom succeeded in correcting anything. I just raised barriers of resentment that cut off any suggestion, example, understanding, or love."

««« »»»

"A.A.'s often say, 'Our leaders do not drive by mandate; they lead by example.' If we would favorably affect others, we ourselves need to practice what we preach—and forget the 'preaching,' too. The quiet good example speaks for itself."

1. LETTER, 1945
2. LETTER, 1966

Meeting Adversity

"Our spiritual and emotional growth in A.A. does not depend so deeply upon success as it does upon our failures and setbacks. If you will bear this in mind, I think that your slip will have the effect of kicking you upstairs, instead of down.

"We A.A.'s have had no better teacher than Old Man Adversity, except in those cases where we refuse to let him teach us."

« « «   » » »

"Now and then all of us fall under heavy criticism. When we are angered and hurt, it's difficult not to retaliate in kind. Yet we can restrain ourselves and then probe ourselves, asking whether our critics were really right. If so, we can admit our defects to them. This usually clears the air for mutual understanding.

"Suppose our critics are being unfair. Then we can try calm persuasion. If they continue to rant, it is still possible for us—in our hearts—to forgive them. Maybe a sense of humor can be our saving grace—thus we can both forgive and forget."

1. LETTER, 1958
2. LETTER, 1966

Boomerang

When I was ten, I was tall and gawky, and smaller kids could push me around in quarrels. I remember being very depressed for a year or more, and then I began to develop a fierce resolve to win.

One day, my grandfather came along with a book about Australia and told me, "This book says that nobody but an Australian bushman knows how to make and throw the boomerang."

"Here's my chance," I thought. "I will be the first man in America to make and throw a boomerang." Well, any kid could have had a notion like that. It might have lasted two days or two weeks. But mine was a power drive that kept on for six months, till I made a boomerang that swung around the church yard in front of the house and almost hit my grandfather in the head when it came back.

Emotionally, I had begun the fashioning of another sort of boomerang, one that almost killed me later on.

"The Only Requirement . . ."

In Tradition Three, A.A. is really saying to every
serious drinker, "You are an A.A. member if
you say so. You can declare yourself in; nobody
can keep you out. No matter how low you've
gone, no matter how grave your emotional com-
plications—even your crimes—we don't want to
keep you out. We just want to be sure that you
get the same chance for sobriety that we've had."

《《《　》》》

We do not wish to deny anyone his chance to
recover from alcoholism. We wish to be just as
inclusive as we can, never exclusive.

1. TWELVE AND TWELVE, P. 139
2. GRAPEVINE, AUGUST 1946

Talk or Action?

In making amends, it is seldom wise to approach an individual who still smarts from our injustice to him, and announce that we have gone religious. This might be called leading with the chin. Why lay ourselves open to being branded fanatics or religious bores? If we do this, we may kill a future opportunity to carry a beneficial message.

But the man who hears our amends is sure to be impressed with our sincere desire to set right a wrong. He is going to be more interested in a demonstration of good will than in talk of spiritual discoveries.

To Survive Trials

In our belief, any scheme of combating alcoholism which proposes wholly to shield the sick man from temptation is doomed to failure. If the alcoholic tries to shield himself he may succeed for a time, but he usually winds up with a bigger explosion than ever. We have tried these methods. These attempts to do the impossible have always failed. Release from alcohol, and not flight from it, is our answer.

«««   »»»

"Faith without works is dead." How appallingly true for the alcoholic! For if an alcoholic fails to perfect and enlarge his spiritual life through work and self-sacrifice for others, he cannot survive the certain trials and low spots ahead. If he does not work, he will surely drink again, and if he drinks, he will surely die. Then faith will be dead indeed.

ALCOHOLICS ANONYMOUS
1. P. 101
2. PP. 14-15

Experimenters

We agnostics liked A.A. all right, and were quick to say that it had done miracles. But we recoiled from meditation and prayer as obstinately as the scientist who refused to perform a certain experiment lest it prove his pet theory wrong.

When we finally did experiment, and unexpected results followed, we felt different; in fact, we knew different; and so we were sold on meditation and prayer. And that, we have found, can happen to anybody who tries. It has been well said that "Almost the only scoffers at prayer are those who never tried it enough."

*The A.A. Way in the Home**

Though an alcoholic does not respond, there is
no reason why you should neglect his family. You
should continue to be friendly to them, explaining
A.A.'s concept of alcoholism and its treatment. If
they accept this and also apply our principles to
their problems, there is a much better chance that
the head of the family will recover. And even
though he continues to drink, the family will find
life more bearable.

«« »»

Unless a new member's family readily expresses a
desire to live upon spiritual principles, we think
he ought not to urge them. They will change in
time. His better behavior will usually convince
them far more than his words.

ALCOHOLICS ANONYMOUS
1. P. 97
2. P. 83

* Today, the initiation of the A.A. way of life in the home is the central
purpose of the Al-Anon Family Groups, of which there are (as of 1984)
over 22,000 throughout the world. These are composed of wives, husbands,
and relatives of alcoholics. In restoring families to the good life, Al-Anon's
success has been enormous.

The Beginning of Humility

"There are few absolutes inherent in the Twelve Steps. Most Steps are open to interpretation, based on the experience and outlook of the individual.

"Consequently, the individual is free to start the Steps at whatever point he can, or will. God, as we understand Him, may be defined as a 'Power greater . . .' or the Higher Power. For thousands of members, the A.A. group itself has been a 'Higher Power' in the beginning. This acknowledgment is easy to make if a newcomer knows that most of the members are sober and he isn't.

"His admission is the beginning of humility—at least the newcomer is willing to disclaim that he himself is God. That's all the start he needs. If, following this achievement, he will relax and practice as many of the Steps as he can, he is sure to grow spiritually."

LETTER, 1966

Carrying the Message

The wonderful energy the Twelfth Step releases, by which it carries our message to the next suffering alcoholic and finally translates the Twelve Steps into action upon all our affairs, is the payoff, the magnificent reality of A.A.

«« »»

Never talk down to an alcoholic from any moral or spiritual hilltop; simply lay out the kit of spiritual tools for his inspection. Show him how they worked with you. Offer him friendship and fellowship.

1. TWELVE AND TWELVE, P. 109
2. ALCOHOLICS ANONYMOUS, P. 95

The Spiritual Alibi

Our first attempts at inventories are apt to prove very unrealistic. I used to be a champ at unrealistic self-appraisal. On certain occasions, I wanted to look only at the part of my life which seemed good. Then I would greatly exaggerate whatever virtues I supposed I had attained. Next I would congratulate myself on the grand job I was doing in A.A.

Naturally this generated a terrible hankering for still more "accomplishments," and still more approval. I was falling straight back into the pattern of my drinking days. Here were the same old goals—power, fame, and applause. Besides, I had the best alibi known—the spiritual alibi. The fact that I really did have a spiritual objective made this utter nonsense seem perfectly right.

GRAPEVINE, JUNE 1961

The Obsession and the Answer

The idea that somehow, some day, he will control and enjoy his drinking is the great obsession of every abnormal drinker. The persistence of this illusion is astonishing. Many pursue it into the gates of insanity or death.

«« »»

Alcoholism, not cancer, was my illness, but what was the difference? Was not alcoholism also a consumer of body and mind? Alcoholism took longer to do its killing, but the result was the same. So, I decided, if there was a great Physician who could cure the alcoholic sickness, I had better seek Him at once.

1. ALCOHOLICS ANONYMOUS, P. 30
2. A.A. COMES OF AGE, P. 61

The Language of the Heart

Why, at this particular point in history, has God chosen to communicate His healing grace to so many of us? Every aspect of this global unfoldment can be related to a single crucial word. The word is "communication." There has been a lifesaving communication among ourselves, with the world around us, and with God.

From the beginning, communication in A.A. has been no ordinary transmission of helpful ideas and attitudes. Because of our kinship in suffering, and because our common means of deliverance are effective for ourselves only when constantly carried to others, our channels of contact have always been charged with the language of the heart.

A.A. TODAY, PP. 7-8

Antidote for Fear

When our failings generate fear, we then have
soul-sickness. This sickness, in turn, generates still
more character defects.

Unreasonable fear that our instincts will not be
satisfied drives us to covet the possessions of
others, to lust for sex and power, to become angry
when our instinctive demands are threatened, to
be envious when the ambitions of others seem to
be realized while ours are not. We eat, drink, and
grab for more of everything than we need, fearing
we shall never have enough. And, with genuine
alarm at the prospect of work, we stay lazy. We
loaf and procrastinate, or at best work grudgingly
and under half steam.

These fears are the termites that ceaselessly devour
the foundations of whatever sort of life we try
to build.

《《《　　》》》

As faith grows, so does inner security. The vast
underlying fear of nothingness commences to
subside. We of A.A. find that our basic antidote
for fear is a spiritual awakening.

1. TWELVE AND TWELVE, P. 49
2. GRAPEVINE, JANUARY 1962

Where Rationalizing Leads

"You know what our genius for rationalization is. If, to ourselves, we fully justify one slip, then our rationalizing propensities are almost sure to justify another one, perhaps with a different set of excuses. But one justification leads to another and presently we are back on the bottle full-time."

«« « »» »

Experience shows, all too often, that even the "controlled" pill-taker may get out of control. The same crazy rationalizations that once characterized his drinking begin to blight his existence. He thinks that if pills can cure insomnia so may they cure his worry.

Our friends the doctors are seldom directly to blame for the dire results we so often experience. It is much too easy for alcoholics to buy these dangerous drugs, and once possessed of them the drinker is often likely to use them without any judgment whatever.

1. LETTER, 1959
2. GRAPEVINE, NOVEMBER 1945

Tell the Public?

"A.A.'s of worldly prominence sometimes say, 'If I tell the public that I am in Alcoholics Anonymous, then that will bring in many others.' Thus they express the belief that our anonymity Tradition is wrong—at least for them.

"They forget that, during their drinking days, prestige and the achievement of worldly ambition were their principal aims. They do not realize that, by breaking anonymity, they are unconsciously pursuing those old and perilous illusions once more. They forget that the keeping of one's anonymity often means a sacrifice of one's desire for power, prestige, and money. They do not see that if these strivings became general in A.A., the course of our whole history would be changed; that we would be sowing the seeds of our own destruction as a society.

"Yet I can happily report that while many of us are tempted—and I have been one—few of us in America actually break our anonymity at the public-media level."

LETTER, 1958

Arrogance and Its Opposite

A very tough-minded prospect was taken to his first A.A. meeting, where two speakers (or maybe lecturers) themed their talks on "God as I understand Him." Their attitude oozed arrogance. In fact, the final speaker got far overboard on his personal theological convictions.

Both were repeating my performance of years before. Implicit in everything they said was the same idea: "Folks, listen to us. We have the only true brand of A.A.—and you'd better get it!"

The new prospect said he'd had it—and he had. His sponsor protested that this wasn't real A.A. But it was too late; nobody could touch him after that.

« « « » » »

I see "humility for today" as a safe and secure stance midway between violent emotional extremes. It is a quiet place where I can keep enough perspective and enough balance to take my next small step up the clearly marked road that points toward eternal values.

GRAPEVINE
1. APRIL, 1961
2. JUNE, 1961

Source of Strength

When World War II broke out, our A.A. dependence on a Higher Power had its first major test. A.A.'s entered the services and were scattered all over the world.

Would they be able to take discipline, stand up under fire, and endure the monotony and misery of war? Would the kind of dependence they had learned in A.A. carry them through?

Well, it did. They had even fewer alcoholic lapses or emotional binges than A.A.'s safe at home did. They were just as capable of endurance and valor as any other soldiers. Whether in Alaska or on the Salerno beachhead, their dependence upon a Higher Power worked.

Far from being a weakness, this dependence was their chief source of strength.

201

Unlimited Choice

Any number of alcoholics are bedeviled by the
dire conviction that if ever they go near A.A.
they will be pressured to conform to some particular brand of faith or theology.

They just don't realize that faith is never an im-
perative for A.A. membership; that sobriety can be
achieved with an easily acceptable minimum of it,
and that our concepts of a Higher Power and
God—as we understand Him—afford everyone
a nearly unlimited choice of spiritual belief and
action.

«« «   » »»

In talking to a prospect, stress the spiritual
feature freely. If the man be agnostic or atheist,
make it emphatic that he does not have to agree
with your conception of God. He can choose any
conception he likes, provided it makes sense
to him.

The main thing is that he be willing to believe in
a Power greater than himself and that he live by
spiritual principles.

1. GRAPEVINE, APRIL 1961
2. ALCOHOLICS ANONYMOUS, P. 93

The Hour of Decision

"Not all large decisions can be well made by simply listing the pros and cons of a given situation, helpful and necessary as this process is. We cannot always depend on what seems to us to be logical. When there is doubt about our logic, we wait upon God and listen for the voice of intuition. If, in meditation, that voice is persistent enough, we may well gain sufficient confidence to act upon that, rather than upon logic.

"If, after an exercise of these two disciplines, we are still uncertain, then we should ask for further guidance and, when possible, defer important decisions for a time. By then, with more knowledge of our situation, logic and intuition may well agree upon a right course.

"But if the decision must be now, let us not evade it through fear. Right or wrong, we can always profit from the experience."

LETTER, 1966

True Tolerance

Gradually we began to be able to accept the other fellow's sins as well as his virtues. We coined the potent and meaningful expression "Let us always love the best in others—and never fear their worst."

《《《　》》》

Finally, we begin to see that all people, including ourselves, are to some extent emotionally ill as well as frequently wrong. When this happens, we approach true tolerance and we see what real love for our fellows actually means.

1. GRAPEVINE, JANUARY 1962
2. TWELVE AND TWELVE, P. 92

The Building of Character

Since most of us are born with an abundance of natural desires, it isn't strange that we often let these far exceed their intended purpose. When they drive us blindly, or we willfully demand that they supply us with more satisfactions or pleasures than are possible or due us, that is the point at which we depart from the degree of perfection that God wishes for us here on earth. That is the measure of our character defects, or, if you wish, of our sins.

If we ask, God will certainly forgive our derelictions. But in no case does He render us white as snow and keep us that way without our cooperation. That is something we are supposed to be willing to work toward ourselves. He asks only that we try as best we know how to make progress in the building of character.

TWELVE AND TWELVE, P. 65

Virtue and Self-Deception

I used to take comfort from an exaggerated belief in my own honesty. My New England kinfolk had taught me the sanctity of all business commitments and contracts, saying, "A man's word is his bond." After this rigorous conditioning, business honesty always came easy; I never flimflammed anyone.

However, this small fragment of readily won virtue did produce some interesting liabilities. I never failed to whip up a fine contempt for those of my fellow Wall Streeters who were prone to shortchange their customers. This was arrogant enough, but the ensuing self-deception proved even worse.

My prized business honesty was presently converted into a comfortable cloak under which I could hide the many serious flaws that beset other departments of my life. Being certain of this one virtue, it was easy to conclude that I had them all. For years on end, this prevented me from taking a good look at myself.

Praying for Others

While praying sincerely, we still may fall into temptation. We form ideas as to what we think God's will is for other people. We say to ourselves, "This one ought to be cured of his fatal malady" or "That one ought to be relieved of his emotional pain," and we pray for these specific things.

Such prayers, of course, are fundamentally good acts, but often they are based upon a supposition that we know God's will for the person for whom we pray. This means that side by side with an earnest prayer there can be a certain amount of presumption and conceit in us.

It is A.A.'s experience that particularly in these cases we ought to pray that God's will, whatever it is, be done for others as well as for ourselves.

The Fellowship's Future

"It seems proved that A.A. can stand on its own feet anywhere and under any conditions. It has outgrown any dependence it might once have had upon the personalities or efforts of a few of the older members like me. New, able, and vigorous people keep coming to the surface, turning up where they are needed. Besides, A.A. has reached enough spiritual maturity to know that its final dependence is upon God."

« « «   » » »

Clearly, our first duty to A.A.'s future is to maintain in full strength what we now have. Only the most vigilant caretaking can assure this. Never should we be lulled into complacent self-satisfaction by the wide acclaim and success that are everywhere ours. This is the subtle temptation which could render us stagnant today, perchance disintegrate us tomorrow. We have always rallied to meet and transcend failure and crisis. Problems have been our stimulants. How well, though, shall we be able to meet the problems of success?

1. LETTER, 1940
2. A.A. TODAY, P. 106

Reason—a Bridge to Faith

We were squarely confronted with the question of faith. We couldn't duck the issue. Some of us had already walked along the bridge of reason toward the desired shore of faith, where friendly hands stretched out in welcome. We were grateful that reason had brought us so far. But, somehow, we couldn't quite step ashore. Perhaps we had been relying too heavily on reason that last mile, and we did not like to lose our support.

Yet, without knowing it, had we not been brought to where we stood by a certain kind of faith? For did we not believe in our own reasoning? Did we not have confidence in our ability to think? What was that but a sort of faith? Yes, we had been faithful, abjectly faithful to the god of reason. So, in one way or another, we discovered that faith had been involved all the time!

Never the Same Again

It was discovered that when one alcoholic had planted in the mind of another the true nature of his malady, that person could never be the same again. Following every spree, he would say to himself, "Maybe those A.A.'s were right." After a few such experiences, often before the onset of extreme difficulties, he would return to us convinced.

«« »»

In the first years, those of us who sobered up in A.A. had been grim and utterly hopeless cases. But then we began to have success with milder alcoholics and even some potential alcoholics. Younger folks appeared. Lots of people turned up who still had jobs, homes, health, and even good social standing.

Of course, it was necessary for these newcomers to hit bottom emotionally. But they did not have to hit every possible bottom in order to admit that they were licked.

1. TWELVE AND TWELVE, PP. 23-24
2. A.A. COMES OF AGE, P. 199

Out of Bondage

At Step Three, many of us said to our Maker, as we understood Him: "God, I offer myself to Thee—to build with me and to do with me as Thou wilt. Relieve me of the bondage of self, that I may better do Thy will. Take away my difficulties, that my transcendence over them may bear witness to those I would help of Thy power, Thy love, and Thy way of life. May I do Thy will always!"

We thought well before taking this Step, making sure we were ready. Then we could commence to abandon ourselves utterly to Him.

Reaching for Humility

We saw we needn't always be bludgeoned and beaten into humility. It could come quite as much from our voluntary reaching for it as it could from unremitting suffering.

«««   »»»

"We first reach for a little humility, knowing that we shall perish of alcoholism if we do not. After a time, though we may still rebel somewhat, we commence to practice humility because this is the right thing to do. Then comes the day when, finally freed in large degree from rebellion, we practice humility because we deeply want it as a way of life."

1. TWELVE AND TWELVE, P. 75
2. LETTER, 1966

Faith and Action

Your prospect's religious education and training may be far superior to yours. In that case, he is going to wonder how you can add anything to what he already knows.

But he will be curious to learn why his convictions have not worked and why yours seem to work so well. He may be an example of the truth that faith alone is insufficient. To be vital, faith must be accompanied by self-sacrifice and unselfish, constructive action.

Admit that he probably knows more about religion than you do, but remind him that, however deep his faith and knowledge, these qualities could not have served him very well, or he would not be asking your help.

《《《　》》》

Dr. Bob did not need me for his spiritual instruction. He had already had more of that than I. What he did need, when we first met, was the deflation at depth and the understanding that only one drunk can give to another. What I needed was the humility of self-forgetfulness and the kinship with another human being of my own kind.

1. ALCOHOLICS ANONYMOUS, P. 93
2. A.A. TODAY, P. 10

Complete the Housecleaning

Time after time, newcomers have tried to keep to themselves shoddy facts about their lives. Trying to avoid the humbling experience of the Fifth Step, they have turned to easier methods. Almost invariably they got drunk. Having persevered with the rest of the program, they wondered why they fell.

We think the reason is that they never completed their housecleaning. They took inventory all right, but hung on to some of the worst items in stock. They only thought they had lost their egoism and fear; they only thought they had humbled themselves. But they had not learned enough of humility, fearlessness, and honesty, in the sense we find it necessary, until they told someone else their entire life story.

Only Try

In my teens, I had to be an athlete because I was not an athlete. I had to be a musician because I could not carry a tune. I had to be the president of my class in boarding school. I had to be first in everything because in my perverse heart I felt myself the least of God's creatures. I could not accept my deep sense of inferiority, and so I strove to become captain of the baseball team, and I did learn to play the fiddle. Lead I must—or else. This was the "all or nothing" kind of demand that later did me in.

«« »»

"I'm glad you are going to try that new job. But make sure that you are only going to 'try.' If you approach the project in the attitude that 'I must succeed, I must not fail, I cannot fail,' then you practically guarantee the flop which in turn will guarantee a drinking relapse. But if you look at the venture as a constructive experiment only, then all should go well."

1. A.A. COMES OF AGE, P. 53
2. LETTER, 1958

Constructive Workouts

There are those in A.A. whom we call "destructive" critics. They power-drive, they are "politickers," they make accusations to gain their ends —all for the good of A.A., of course! But we have learned that these folks need not be really destructive.

We ought to listen carefully to what they say. Sometimes they are telling the whole truth; at other times, a little truth. If we are within their range, the whole truth, the half-truth, or no truth at all can prove equally unpleasant to us. If they have got the whole truth, or even a little truth, then we had better thank them and get on with our respective inventories, admitting we were wrong. If they are talking nonsense, we can ignore it, or else try to persuade them. Failing this, we can be sorry they are too sick to listen, and we can try to forget the whole business.

There are few better means of self-survey and of developing patience than the workouts these usually well-meaning but erratic members so often afford us.

TWELVE CONCEPTS, P. 40

After the "Honeymoon"

"For most of us, the first years of A.A. are something like a honeymoon. There is a new and potent reason to stay alive, joyful activity aplenty. For a time, we are diverted from the main life problems. That is all to the good.

"But when the honeymoon has worn off, we are obliged to take our lumps, like other people. This is where the testing starts. Maybe the group has pushed us onto the side lines. Maybe difficulties have intensified at home, or in the world outside. Then the old behavior patterns reappear. How well we recognize and deal with them reveals the extent of our progress."

«« »»

The wise have always known that no one can make much of his life until self-searching becomes a regular habit, until he is able to admit and accept what he finds, and until he patiently and persistently tries to correct what is wrong.

1. LETTER, 1954
2. TWELVE AND TWELVE, P. 88

Hope Born from Hopelessness

Letter to Dr. Carl Jung:

"Most conversion experiences, whatever their variety, do have a common denominator of ego collapse at depth. The individual faces an impossible dilemma.

"In my case the dilemma had been created by my compulsive drinking, and the deep feeling of hopelessness had been vastly deepened by my doctor. It was deepened still more by my alcoholic friend when he acquainted me with your verdict of hopelessness respecting Rowland H.

"In the wake of my spiritual experience there came a vision of a society of alcoholics. If each sufferer were to carry the news of the scientific hopelessness of alcoholism to each new prospect, he might be able to lay every newcomer wide open to a transforming spiritual experience. This concept proved to be the foundation of such success as A.A. has since achieved."

Happy—When We're Free

For most normal folks, drinking means release
from care, boredom, and worry. It means joyous
intimacy with friends and a feeling that life
is good.

But not so with us in those last days of heavy
drinking. The old pleasures were gone. There was
an insistent yearning to enjoy life as we once
did and a heartbreaking delusion that some new
miracle of control would enable us to do it. There
was always one more attempt—and one more
failure.

«« »»

We are sure God would like to see us happy,
joyous, and free. Hence, we cannot subscribe to
the belief that this life necessarily has to be a
vale of tears, though it once was just that for
many of us. But it became clear that most of the
time we had made our own misery.

ALCOHOLICS ANONYMOUS
1. P. 151
2. P. 133

Willing to Believe

Do not let any prejudice you may have against spiritual terms deter you from honestly asking yourself what they might mean to you. At the start, this was all we needed to commence spiritual growth, to effect our first conscious relation with God as we understood Him. Afterward, we found ourselves accepting many things which had seemed entirely out of reach. That was growth. But if we wished to grow we had to begin somewhere. So at first we used our own conceptions of God, however limited they were.

We needed to ask ourselves but one short question: "Do I now believe, or am I even willing to believe, that there is a Power greater than myself?" As soon as a man can say that he does believe, even in this small degree, or is willing to believe, we emphatically assure him that he is on his way.

In Partnership

As we made spiritual progress, it became clear that, if we ever were to feel emotionally secure, we would have to put our lives on a give-and-take basis; we would have to develop the sense of being in partnership or brotherhood with all those around us. We saw that we would need to give constantly of ourselves without demand for repayment. When we persistently did this, we gradually found that people were attracted to us as never before. And even if they failed us, we could be understanding and not too seriously affected.

«««   »»»

The unity, the effectiveness, and even the survival of A.A. will always depend upon our continued willingness to give up some of our personal ambitions and desires for the common safety and welfare. Just as sacrifice means survival for the individual alcoholic, so does sacrifice mean unity and survival for the group and for A.A.'s entire Fellowship.

1. TWELVE AND TWELVE, PP. 115-116
2. A.A. COMES OF AGE, PP. 287-288

God Will Not Desert Us

"Word comes to me that you are making a magnificent stand in adversity—this adversity being the state of your health. It gives me a chance to express my gratitude for your recovery in A.A. and especially for the demonstration of its principles you are now so inspiringly giving to us all.

"You will be glad to know that A.A.'s have an almost unfailing record in this respect. This, I think, is because we are so aware that God will not desert us when the chips are down; indeed, He did not when we were drinking. And so it should be with the remainder of life.

"Certainly, He does not plan to save us from all troubles and adversity. Nor, in the end, does He save us from so-called death—since this is but an opening of a door into a new life, where we shall dwell among His many mansions. Touching these things I know you have a most confident faith."

LETTER, 1966

Who Is to Blame?

At Step Four we resolutely looked for our own mistakes. Where had we been selfish, dishonest, self-seeking, and frightened? Though a given situation had not been entirely our fault, we often tried to cast the whole blame on the other person involved.

We finally saw that the inventory should be ours, not the other man's. So we admitted our wrongs honestly and became willing to set these matters straight.

ALCOHOLICS ANONYMOUS, P. 67

One Fellowship—Many Faiths

As a society we must never become so vain as to suppose that we are authors and inventors of a new religion. We will humbly reflect that every one of A.A.'s principles has been borrowed from ancient sources.

«« «   » »»

A minister in Thailand wrote, "We took A.A.'s Twelve Steps to the largest Buddhist monastery in this province, and the head priest said, 'Why, these Steps are fine! For us as Buddhists, it might be slightly more acceptable if you had inserted the word 'good' in your Steps instead of 'God.' Nevertheless, you say that it is God as you understand Him, and that must certainly include the good. Yes, A.A.'s Twelve Steps will surely be accepted by the Buddhists around here.' "

«« «   » »»

St. Louis oldtimers recall how Father Edward Dowling helped start their group; it turned out to be largely Protestant, but this fazed him not a bit.

A.A. COMES OF AGE
1. P. 231
2. P. 81
3. P. 37

Leadership in A.A.

No society can function well without able leadership at all its levels, and A.A. can be no exception. But we A.A.'s sometimes cherish the thought that we can do without much personal leadership at all. We are apt to warp the traditional idea of "principles before personalities" around to such a point that there would be no "personality" in leadership whatever. This would imply rather faceless robots trying to please everybody.

A leader in A.A. service is a man (or woman) who can personally put principles, plans, and policies into such dedicated and effective action that the rest of us naturally want to back him up and help him with his job. When a leader power-drives us badly, we rebel; but when he too meekly becomes an order-taker and he exercises no judgment of his own—well, he really isn't a leader at all.

TWELVE CONCEPTS, PP. 38–39

The Answer in the Mirror

While drinking, we were certain that our intelligence, backed by will power, could rightly control our inner lives and guarantee us success in the world around us. This brave philosophy, wherein each man played God, sounded good in the speaking, but it still had to meet the acid test: How well did it actually work? One good look in the mirror was answer enough.

«« »»

My spiritual awakening was electrically sudden and absolutely convincing. At once I became a part—if only a tiny part—of a cosmos that was ruled by justice and love in the person of God. No matter what had been the consequences of my own willfulness and ignorance, or those of my fellow travelers on earth, this was still the truth. Such was the new and positive assurance, and this has never left me.

1. TWELVE AND TWELVE, P. 37
2. GRAPEVINE, JANUARY 1962

Humility for the Fellowship, Too

We of A.A. sometimes brag of the virtues of our
Fellowship. Let us remember that few of these are
actually earned virtues. We were forced into
them, to begin with, by the cruel lash of alcoholism. We finally adopted them, not because
we wished to, but because we had to.

Then, as time confirmed the seeming rightness of
our basic principles, we began to conform because
it was right to do so. Some of us, notably
myself, conformed even then with reluctance.

But at last we came to a point where we stood
willing to conform gladly to the principles which
experience, under the grace of God, had taught us.

A.A. COMES OF AGE, P. 224

Is Sobriety Enough?

The alcoholic is like a tornado roaring his way through the lives of others. Hearts are broken. Sweet relationships are dead. Affections have been uprooted. Selfish and inconsiderate habits have kept the home in turmoil.

We feel a man is unthinking when he says that sobriety is enough. He is like the farmer who came up out of his cyclone cellar to find his home ruined. To his wife, he remarked, "Don't see anything the matter here, Ma. Ain't it grand the wind stopped blowin'?"

《《《　》》》

We ask ourselves what we mean when we say that we have "harmed" other people. What kinds of "harm" do people do one another, anyway? To define the word "harm" in a practical way, we might call it the result of instincts in collision, which cause physical, mental, emotional, or spiritual damage to those about us.

1. ALCOHOLICS ANONYMOUS, P. 82
2. TWELVE AND TWELVE, P. 80

The Beginning of True Kinship

When we reached A.A., and for the first time in our lives stood among people who seemed to understand, the sense of belonging was tremendously exciting. We thought the isolation problem had been solved.

But we soon discovered that, while we weren't alone any more in a social sense, we still suffered many of the old pangs of anxious apartness. Until we had talked with complete candor of our conflicts, and had listened to someone else do the same thing, we still didn't belong.

Step Five was the answer. It was the beginning of true kinship with man and God.

Day of Homecoming

"As sobriety means long life and happiness for the individual, so does unity mean exactly the same thing to our Society as a whole. Unified we live; disunited we shall perish."

«« »»

"We must think deeply of all those sick ones still to come to A.A. As they try to make their return to faith and to life, we want them to find everything in A.A. that we have found, and yet more, if that be possible. No care, no vigilance, no effort to preserve A.A.'s constant effectiveness and spiritual strength will ever be too great to hold us in full readiness for the day of their homecoming."

1. LETTER, 1949
2. TALK, 1959

Love Everybody?

Not many people can truthfully assert that they love everybody. Most of us must admit that we have loved but a few; that we have been quite indifferent to the many. As for the remainder— well, we have really disliked or hated them.

We A.A.'s find we need something much better than this in order to keep our balance. The idea that we can be possessively loving of a few, can ignore the many, and can continue to fear or hate anybody at all, has to be abandoned, if only a little at a time.

We can try to stop making unreasonable demands upon those we love. We can show kindness where we had formerly shown none. With those we dislike we can at least begin to practice justice and courtesy, perhaps going out of our way at times to understand and help them.

TWELVE AND TWELVE, PP. 92-93

Privileged to Communicate

Everyone must agree that we A.A.'s are unbelievably fortunate people; fortunate that we have suffered so much; fortunate that we can know, understand, and love each other so supremely well.

These attributes and virtues are scarcely of the earned variety. Indeed, most of us are well aware that these are rare gifts which have their true origin in our kinship born of a common suffering and a common deliverance by the grace of God.

Thereby we are privileged to communicate with each other to a degree and in a manner not very often surpassed among our nonalcoholic friends in the world around us.

« « «   » » »

"I used to be ashamed of my condition and so didn't talk about it. But nowadays I freely confess I am a depressive, and this has attracted other depressives to me. Working with them has helped a great deal."*

1. GRAPEVINE, OCTOBER 1959
2. LETTER, 1954
* Bill added that he had no depression after 1955.

The Value of Human Will

Many newcomers, having experienced little but constant deflation, feel a growing conviction that human will is of no value whatever. They have become persuaded, sometimes rightly so, that many problems besides alcohol will not yield to a headlong assault powered only by the individual's will.

However, there are certain things which the individual alone can do. All by himself, and in the light of his own circumstances, he needs to develop the quality of willingness. When he acquires willingness, he is the only one who can then make the decision to exert himself along spiritual lines. Trying to do this is actually an act of his own will. It is a right use of this faculty.

Indeed, all of A.A.'s Twelve Steps require our sustained and personal exertion to conform to their principles and so, we trust, to God's will.

Everyday Living

The A.A. emphasis on personal inventory is heavy because a great many of us have never really acquired the habit of accurate self-appraisal.

Once this healthy practice has become a habit, it will prove so interesting and profitable that the time it takes won't be missed. For these minutes and often hours spent in self-examination are bound to make all the other hours of our day better and happier. At length, our inventories become a necessity of everyday living, rather than something unusual or set apart.

TWELVE AND TWELVE, PP. 89-90

Freed Prisoners

Letter to a prison group:

"Every A.A. has been, in a sense, a prisoner. Each of us has walled himself out of society; each has known social stigma. The lot of you folks has been even more difficult: In your case, society has also built a wall around you. But there isn't any really essential difference, a fact that practically all A.A.'s now know.

"Therefore, when you members come into the world of A.A. on the outside, you can be sure that no one will care a fig that you have done time. What you are trying to be—not what you were—is all that counts with us."

« « «   » » »

"Mental and emotional difficulties are sometimes very hard to take while we are trying to maintain sobriety. Yet we do see, in the long run, that transcendence over such problems is the real test of the A.A. way of living. Adversity gives us more opportunity to grow than does comfort or success."

1. LETTER, 1949
2. LETTER, 1964

Looking for Lost Faith

Any number of A.A.'s can say, "We were diverted from our childhood faith. As material success began to come, we felt we were winning at the game of life. This was exhilarating, and it made us happy.

"Why should we be bothered with theological abstractions and religious duties, or with the state of our souls, here or hereafter? The will to win should carry us through.

"But then alcohol began to have its way with us. Finally, when all our score cards read 'zero,' and we saw that one more strike would put us out of the game forever, we had to look for our lost faith. It was in A.A. that we rediscovered it."

TWELVE AND TWELVE, PP. 28-29

Perfection—Only the Objective

There can be no absolute humility for us humans.
At best, we can merely glimpse the meaning and
splendor of such a perfect ideal. Only God
himself can manifest in the absolute; we human
beings must needs live and grow in the domain
of the relative.

So we seek progress in humility for today.

«‹«   »›»

Few of us can quickly or easily become ready
even to look at spiritual and moral perfection; we
want to settle for only as much development as
may get us by in life, according, of course,
to our various and sundry ideas of what will get us
by. Mistakenly, we strive for a self-determined
objective, rather than for the perfect objective
which is of God.

1. GRAPEVINE, JUNE 1961
2. TWELVE AND TWELVE, P. 68

No Orders Issued

Neither the A.A. General Service Conference, its Board of Trustees, nor the humblest group committee can issue a single directive to an A.A. member and make it stick, let alone mete out any punishment. We've tried this lots of times, but utter failure is always the result.

Groups have sometimes tried to expel members, but the banished have come back to sit in the meeting place, saying, "This is life for us; you can't keep us out." Committees have instructed many an A.A. to stop working on a chronic backslider, only to be told: "How I do my Twelfth Step work is my business. Who are you to judge?"

This doesn't mean that an A.A. won't take good advice or suggestions from more experienced members. He simply objects to taking orders.

TWELVE AND TWELVE, P. 173

Maudlin Martyrdom

"Self-pity is one of the most unhappy and consuming defects that we know. It is a bar to all spiritual progress and can cut off all effective communication with our fellows because of its inordinate demands for attention and sympathy. It is a maudlin form of martyrdom, which we can ill afford.

"The remedy? Well, let's have a hard look at ourselves, and a still harder one at A.A.'s Twelve Steps to recovery. When we see how many of our fellow A.A.'s have used the Steps to transcend great pain and adversity, we shall be inspired to try these life-giving principles for ourselves."

LETTER, 1966

When and How to Give

Men who cry for money and shelter as a condition of their sobriety are on the wrong track. Yet we sometimes do provide a new prospect with these very things—when it becomes clear that he is willing to place his recovery first.

It is not whether we shall give that is the question, but when and how to give. Whenever we put our work on a material plane, the alcoholic commences to rely upon alms rather than upon a Higher Power and the A.A. group. He continues to insist that he cannot master alcohol until his material needs are cared for.

Nonsense! Some of us have taken very hard knocks to learn this truth: that, job or no job, wife or no wife, we simply do not stop drinking so long as we place material dependence upon other people ahead of dependence on God.

Hard on Ourselves, Considerate of Others

We cannot disclose anything to our wives or our parents which will hurt them and make them unhappy. We have no right to save our own skins at their expense.

Such damaging parts of our story we tell to someone else who will understand, yet be unaffected. The rule is, we must be hard on ourselves, but always considerate of others.

Good judgment will suggest that we ought to take our time in making amends to our families. It may be unwise at first to rehash certain harrowing episodes. While we may be quite willing to reveal the very worst, we must be sure to remember that we cannot buy our own peace of mind at the expense of others.

1. ALCOHOLICS ANONYMOUS, P. 74
2. TWELVE AND TWELVE, P. 84

Middle of the Road

"In some sections of A.A., anonymity is carried
to the point of real absurdity. Members are on
such a poor basis of communication that they
don't even know each other's last names or where
each lives. It's like the cell of an underground.

"In other sections, we see exactly the reverse. It
is difficult to restrain A.A.'s from shouting too
much before the whole public, by going on
spectacular 'lecture tours' to play the big shot.

"However, I know that from these extremes we
slowly pull ourselves onto a middle ground. Most
lecture-giving members do not last too long,
and the superanonymous people are apt to come
out of hiding respecting their A.A. friends, business associates, and the like. I think the long-time
trend is toward the middle of the road—which is
probably where we should be."

LETTER, 1959

Let Go Absolutely

After failure on my part to dry up any drunks, Dr. Silkworth reminded me of Professor William James's observation that truly transforming spiritual experiences are nearly always founded on calamity and collapse. "Stop preaching at them," Dr. Silkworth said, "and give them the hard medical facts first. This may soften them up at depth so that they will be willing to do anything to get well. Then they may accept those spiritual ideas of yours, and even a Higher Power."

« « «   » » »

We beg of you to be fearless and thorough from the very start. Some of us have tried to hold on to our old ideas, and the result was nil—until we let go absolutely.

1. A.A. COMES OF AGE, P. 13
2. ALCOHOLICS ANONYMOUS, P. 58

Morning Thoughts

On awakening, let us think about the twenty-four hours ahead. We ask God to direct our thinking, especially asking that it be divorced from self-pity and from dishonest or self-seeking motives. Free of these, we can employ our mental faculties with assurance, for God gave us brains to use. Our thought-life will be on a higher plane when our thinking begins to be cleared of wrong motives.

If we have to determine which of two courses to take, we ask God for inspiration, an intuitive thought, or a decision. Then we relax and take it easy, and we are often surprised how the right answers come after we have tried this for a while.

We usually conclude our meditation with a prayer that we be shown all through the day what our next step is to be, asking especially for freedom from damaging self-will.

ALCOHOLICS ANONYMOUS, PP. 86, 87

Toward Maturity

Many oldsters who have put our A.A. "booze
cure" to severe but successful tests still find
they often lack emotional sobriety. To attain this,
we must develop real maturity and balance (which
is to say, humility) in our relations with
ourselves, with our fellows, and with God.

《《《   》》》

Let A.A. never be a closed corporation; let us
never deny our experience, for whatever it may be
worth, to the world around us. Let our individual
members heed the call to every field of human
endeavor. Let them carry the experience and
spirit of A.A. into all these affairs, for whatever
good they may accomplish. For not only has God
saved us from alcoholism; the world has
received us back into its citizenship.

1. GRAPEVINE, JANUARY 1958
2. A.A. COMES OF AGE, PP. 232-233

Singlehanded Combat

Few indeed are those who, assailed by the tyrant
alcohol, have ever won through in singlehanded
combat. It is a statistical fact that alcoholics
almost never recover on their personal resources
alone.

«« »»

'Way up toward Point Barrow in Alaska, a couple
of prospectors got themselves a cabin and a case
of Scotch. The weather turned bitter, fifty
below, and they got so drunk they let the fire go
out. Barely escaping death by freezing, one of
them woke up in time to rekindle the fire.
He was prowling around outside for fuel, and he
looked into an empty oil drum filled with frozen
water. Down in the ice cake he saw a reddish-
yellow object. When thawed out, it was seen to be
an A.A. book. One of the pair read the book
and sobered up. Legend has it that he became
the founder of one of our farthest north groups.

1. TWELVE AND TWELVE, P. 22
2. A.A. COMES OF AGE, PP. 82-83

Instinct to Live

When men and women pour so much alcohol into themselves that they destroy their lives, they commit a most unnatural act. Defying their instinctive desire for self-preservation, they seem bent upon self-destruction. They work against their own deepest instinct.

As they are progressively humbled by the terrific beating administered by alcohol, the grace of God can enter them and expel their obsession. Here their powerful instinct to live can cooperate fully with their Creator's desire to give them new life.

«« »»

"The central characteristic of the spiritual experience is that it gives the recipient a new and better motivation out of all proportion to any process of discipline, belief, or faith.

"These experiences cannot make us whole at once; they are a rebirth to a fresh and certain opportunity."

1. TWELVE AND TWELVE, P. 64
2. LETTER, 1965

Have You Experimented?

"Since open-mindedness and experimentation are supposed to be the indispensable attributes of our 'scientific' civilization, it seems strange that so many scientists are reluctant to try out personally the hypothesis that God came first and man afterward. They prefer to believe that man is the chance product of evolution; that God, the Creator, does not exist.

"I can only report that I have experimented with both concepts and that, in my case, the God concept has proved to be a better basis for living than the man-centered one.

"Nevertheless, I would be the first to defend your right to think as you will. I simply ask this question: 'In your own life, have you ever really tried to think and act as though there might be a God? Have you experimented?' "

LETTER, 1950

We Need Outside Help

It was evident that a solitary self-appraisal, and the admission of our defects based upon that alone, wouldn't be nearly enough. We'd have to have outside help if we were surely to know and admit the truth about ourselves—the help of God and of another human being.

Only by discussing ourselves, holding back nothing, only by being willing to take advice and accept direction could we set foot on the road to straight thinking, solid honesty, and genuine humility.

«« »»

If we are fooling ourselves, a competent adviser can see this quickly. And, as he skillfully guides us away from our fantasies, we are surprised to find that we have few of the usual urges to defend ourselves against unpleasant truths. In no other way can fear, pride, and ignorance be so readily melted. After a time, we realize that we are standing firm on a brand-new foundation for integrity, and we gratefully credit our sponsors, whose advice pointed the way.

1. TWELVE AND TWELVE, P. 59
2. GRAPEVINE, AUGUST 1961

God's Gifts

We see that the sun never sets upon A.A.'s Fellowship; that more than three hundred and fifty thousand of us have now recovered from our malady; that we have everywhere begun to transcend the formidable barriers of race, creed, and nationality. This assurance that so many of us have been able to meet our responsibilities for sobriety and for growth and effectiveness in the troubled world where we live, will surely fill us with the deepest joy and satisfaction.

But, as a people who have nearly always learned the hard way, we shall certainly not congratulate ourselves. We shall perceive these assets to be God's gifts, which have been in part matched by an increasing willingness on our part to find and do His will for us.

Prayer Under Pressure

Whenever I find myself under acute tensions, I lengthen my daily walks and slowly repeat our Serenity Prayer in rhythm to my steps and breathing.

If I feel that my pain has in part been occasioned by others, I try to repeat, "God grant me the serenity to love their best, and never fear their worst." This benign healing process of repetition, sometimes necessary to persist with for days, has seldom failed to restore me to at least a workable emotional balance and perspective.

Face the Music

"Don't be too discouraged about that slip.
Practically always, we drunks learn the hard way.

"Your idea of moving on to somewhere else may
be good, or it may not. Perhaps you have got into
an emotional or economic jam that can't be
well handled where you are. But maybe you are
doing just what all of us have done, at one
time or another: Maybe you are running away.
Why don't you try to think that through again
carefully?

"Are you really placing recovery first, or are you
making it contingent upon other people, places,
or circumstances? You may find it ever so much
better to face the music right where you are
now, and, with the help of the A.A. program, win
through. Before you make a decision, weigh it
in these terms."

LETTER, 1949

Alone No More

Alcoholism was a lonely business, even though we were surrounded by people who loved us. But when our self-will had driven everybody away and our isolation became complete, we commenced to play the big shot in cheap barrooms. Failing even in this, we had to fare forth alone on the street to depend upon the charity of passers-by.

We were trying to find emotional security either by dominating or by being dependent upon others. Even when our fortunes had not totally ebbed, we nevertheless found ourselves alone in the world. We still vainly tried to be secure by some unhealthy sort of domination or dependence.

For those of us who were like that, A.A. has a very special meaning. In this Fellowship we begin to learn right relations with people who understand us; we don't have to be alone any more.

TWELVE AND TWELVE, PP. 116-117

"Look Before You Leap"?

"Wise men and women rightly give a top rating to the virtue of prudence. They know that without this all important attribute little wisdom is to be had.

"Mere 'looking before we leap' is not enough. If our looking is charged with fear, suspicion, or anger, we had better not have looked or acted at all."

《 《 《   》 》 》

"We lose the fear of making decisions, great and small, as we realize that should our choice prove wrong we can, if we will, learn from the experience. Should our decision be the right one, we can thank God for giving us the courage and the grace that caused us so to act."

LETTERS, 1966

Satisfactions of Right Living

How wonderful is the feeling that we do not have
to be specially distinguished among our fellows
in order to be useful and profoundly happy. Not
many of us can be leaders of prominence, nor
do we wish to be.

Service gladly rendered, obligations squarely met,
troubles well accepted or solved with God's help,
the knowledge that at home or in the world
outside we are partners in a common effort, the
fact that in God's sight all human beings are
important, the proof that love freely given brings
a full return, the certainty that we are no longer
isolated and alone in self-constructed prisons,
the surety that we can fit and belong in God's
scheme of things—these are the satisfactions of
right living for which no pomp and circumstance,
no heap of material possessions, could possibly be
substitutes.

Wider Understanding

To reach more alcoholics, understanding of A.A.
and public good will towards A.A. must go on
growing everywhere. We need to be on still better
terms with medicine, religion, employers, govern-
ments, courts, prisons, mental hospitals, and
all enterprises in the alcoholism field. We need
the increasing good will of editors, writers,
television and radio channels. These publicity
outlets need to be opened ever wider.

«««   »»»

Nothing matters more to A.A.'s future welfare
than the manner in which we use the colossus
of modern communication. Used unselfishly and
well, it can produce results surpassing our present
imagination.

Should we handle this great instrument badly, we
shall be shattered by the ego manifestations of
our own people. Against this peril, A.A. members'
anonymity before the general public is our
shield and our buckler.

1. TWELVE CONCEPTS, P. 51
2. GRAPEVINE, NOVEMBER 1960

A "Special" Experience?

I was the recipient of a tremendous mystic experience or "illumination," and at first it was very natural for me to feel that this experience staked me out as somebody very special.

But as I now look back upon this tremendous event, I can only feel very grateful. It now seems clear that the only special features of my experience were its suddenness and the overwhelming and immediate conviction that it carried.

In all other respects, however, I am sure that my own experience was essentially like that received by any A.A. member who has strenuously practiced our recovery program. Surely, the grace he receives is also of God; the only difference is that he becomes aware of his gift more gradually.

Key to Sobriety

The unique ability of each A.A. to identify himself with, and bring recovery to, the newcomer in no way depends upon his learning, his eloquence, or any special individual skills. The only thing that matters is that he is an alcoholic who has found a key to sobriety.

《《《　》》》

In my first conversation with Dr. Bob, I bore down heavily on the medical hopelessness of his case, freely using Dr. Silkworth's words describing the alcoholic's dilemma, the "obsession plus allergy" theme. Though Bob was a doctor, this was news to him, bad news. And the fact that I was an alcoholic and knew what I was talking about from personal experience made the blow a shattering one.

You see, our talk was a completely mutual thing. I had quit preaching. I knew that I needed this alcoholic as much as he needed me.

1. TWELVE AND TWELVE, PP. 150-151
2. A.A. COMES OF AGE, PP. 69-70

Beneath the Surface

Some will object to many of the questions that should be answered in a moral inventory, because they think their own character defects have not been so glaring. To these, it can be suggested that a conscientious examination is likely to reveal the very defects the objectionable questions are concerned with.

Because our surface record hasn't looked too bad, we have frequently been abashed to find that this is so simply because we have buried these selfsame defects deep down in us under thick layers of self-justification. Those were the defects that finally ambushed us into alcoholism and misery.

TWELVE AND TWELVE, PP. 53-54

Servant, Not Master

In A.A., we found that it did not matter too much what our material condition was, but it mattered greatly what our spiritual condition was. As we improved our spiritual outlook, money gradually became our servant and not our master. It became a means of exchanging love and service with those about us.

«« »»

One of A.A.'s Loners is an Australian sheepman who lives two thousand miles from the nearest town, where yearly he sells his wool. In order to be paid the best prices he has to get to town during a certain month. But when he heard that a big regional A.A. meeting was to be held at a later date when wool prices would have fallen, he gladly took a heavy financial loss in order to make his journey then. That's how much an A.A. meeting means to him.

1. TWELVE AND TWELVE, P. 122
2. A.A. COMES OF AGE, P. 31

Inward Reality

It is being constantly revealed, as mankind studies the material world, that its outward appearance is not inward reality at all. The prosaic steel girder is a mass of electrons whirling around each other at incredible speed, and these tiny bodies are governed by precise laws. Science tells us so. We have no reason to doubt it.

When, however, the perfectly logical assumption is suggested that, infinitely beyond the material world as we see it, there is an all powerful, guiding, creative Intelligence, our perverse streak comes to the surface and we set out to convince ourselves that this isn't so. Were our contention true, it would follow that life originated out of nothing, means nothing, and proceeds nowhere.

"Fearless and Searching"

My self-analysis has frequently been faulty.
Sometimes I've failed to share my defects with the
right people; at other times, I've confessed their
defects, rather than my own; and at still other
times, my confession of defects has been more in
the nature of loud complaints about my circumstances and my problems.

« « «   » » »

When A.A. suggests a fearless moral inventory, it
must seem to every newcomer that more is being
asked of him than he can do. Every time he
tries to look within himself, Pride says, "You need
not pass this way," and Fear says, "You dare
not look!"

But pride and fear of this sort turn out to be
bogymen, nothing else. Once we have a complete
willingness to take inventory, and exert ourselves
to do the job thoroughly, a wonderful light falls
upon this foggy scene. As we persist, a brand-
new kind of confidence is born, and the sense of
relief at finally facing ourselves is indescribable.

1. GRAPEVINE, JUNE 1958
2. TWELVE AND TWELVE, PP. 49-50

Individual Responsibilities

Let us emphasize that our reluctance to fight one another, or anybody else, is not counted as some special virtue which entitles us A.A.'s to feel superior to other people. Nor does this reluctance mean that the members of A.A. are going to back away from their individual responsibilities as citizens. Here they should feel free to act as they see the right upon the public issues of our times.

But when it comes to A.A. as a whole, that's quite a different matter. As a group we do not enter into public controversy, because we are sure that our Society will perish if we do.

Fear and Faith

The achievement of freedom from fear is a lifetime undertaking, one that can never be wholly completed.

When under heavy attack, acute illness, or in other conditions of serious insecurity, we shall all react to this emotion—well or badly, as the case may be. Only the self-deceived will claim perfect freedom from fear.

«‹« »›»

We finally saw that faith in some kind of God was a part of our make-up. Sometimes we had to search persistently, but He was there. He was as much a fact as we were. We found the Great Reality deep down within us.

1. GRAPEVINE, JANUARY 1962
2. ALCOHOLICS ANONYMOUS, P. 55

The Step That Keeps Us Growing

Sometimes, when friends tell us how well we are doing, we know better inside. We know we aren't doing well enough. We still can't handle life, as life is. There must be a serious flaw somewhere in our spiritual practice and development.

What, then, is it?

The chances are better than even that we shall locate our trouble in our misunderstanding or neglect of A.A.'s Step Eleven—prayer, meditation, and the guidance of God.

The other Steps can keep most of us sober and somehow functioning. But Step Eleven can keep us growing, if we try hard and work at it continually.

GRAPEVINE, JUNE 1958

Neither Dependence nor Self-Sufficiency

When we insisted, like infants, that people protect and take care of us or that the world owed us a living, then the result was unfortunate. The people we most loved often pushed us aside or perhaps deserted us entirely. Our disillusionment was hard to bear.

We failed to see that, though adult in years, we were still behaving childishly, trying to turn everybody—friends, wives, husbands, even the world itself—into protective parents. We refused to learn that overdependence upon people is unsuccessful because all people are fallible, and even the best of them will sometimes let us down, especially when our demands for attention become unreasonable.

«« « » » »

We are now on a different basis: the basis of trusting and relying upon God. We trust infinite God rather than our finite selves. Just to the extent that we do as we think He would have us do, and humbly rely on Him, does He enable us to match calamity with serenity.

1. TWELVE AND TWELVE, P. 115
2. ALCOHOLICS ANONYMOUS, P. 68

Give Thanks

Though I still find it difficult to accept today's pain and anxiety with any great degree of serenity—as those more advanced in the spiritual life seem able to do—I can give thanks for present pain nevertheless.

I find the willingness to do this by contemplating the lessons learned from past suffering—lessons which have led to the blessings I now enjoy. I can remember how the agonies of alcoholism, the pain of rebellion and thwarted pride, have often led me to God's grace, and so to a new freedom.

Behind Our Excuses

As excuse-makers and rationalizers, we drunks are
champions. It is the business of the psychiatrist to
find the deeper causes for our conduct. Though
uninstructed in psychiatry, we can, after a little
time in A.A., see that our motives have not been
what we thought they were, and that we have
been motivated by forces previously unknown to
us. Therefore we ought to look, with the deepest
respect, interest, and profit, upon the example
set us by psychiatry.

«« »»

"Spiritual growth through the practice of A.A.'s
Twelve Steps, plus the aid of a good sponsor,
can usually reveal most of the deeper reasons for
our character defects, at least to a degree that
meets our practical needs. Nevertheless, we
should be grateful that our friends in psychiatry
have so strongly emphasized the necessity to
search for false and often unconscious
motivations."

1. A.A. COMES OF AGE, P. 236
2. LETTER, 1966

Those Other People

"Just like you, I have often thought myself the victim of what other people say and do. Yet every time I confessed the sins of such people, especially those whose sins did not correspond exactly with my own, I found that I only increased the total damage. My own resentment, my self-pity would often render me well-nigh useless to anybody.

"So, nowadays, if anyone talks of me so as to hurt, I first ask myself if there is any truth at all in what they say. If there is none, I try to remember that I too have had my periods of speaking bitterly of others; that hurtful gossip is but a symptom of our remaining emotional illness; and consequently that I must never be angry at the unreasonableness of sick people.

"Under very trying conditions I have had, again and again, to forgive others—also myself. Have you recently tried this?"

LETTER, 1946

When Infancy Is Over

"You must remember that every A.A. group starts, as it should, through the efforts of a single man and his friends—a founder and his hierarchy. There is no other way.

"But when infancy is over, the original leaders always have to make way for that democracy which springs up through the grass roots and will eventually sweep aside the self-chosen leadership of the past."

《《《   》》》

Letter to Dr. Bob:
"Everywhere the A.A. groups have taken their service affairs into their own hands. Local founders and their friends are now on the side lines. Why so many people forget that, when thinking of the future of our world services, I shall never understand.

"The groups will eventually take over, and maybe they will squander their inheritance when they get it. It is probable, however, that they won't. Anyhow, they really have grown up; A.A. is theirs; let's give it to them."

LETTERS
1. 1950
2. 1949

Honesty and Recovery

In taking an inventory, a member might consider
questions such as these:

How did my selfish pursuit of the sex relation
damage other people and me? What people were
hurt, and how badly? Just how did I react at the
time? Did I burn with guilt? Or did I insist that I
was the pursued and not the pursuer, and thus
absolve myself?

How have I reacted to frustration in sexual
matters? When denied, did I become vengeful or
depressed? Did I take it out on other people? If
there was rejection or coldness at home, did I use
this as a reason for promiscuity?

«« »»

Let no alcoholic say he cannot recover unless he
has his family back. His recovery is not dependent
upon people. It is dependent upon his relationship
with God, however he may define Him.

1. TWELVE AND TWELVE, PP. 50-51
2. ALCOHOLICS ANONYMOUS, PP. 99-100

A.A. in Two Words

"All A.A. progress can be reckoned in terms of just two words: humility and responsibility. Our whole spiritual development can be accurately measured by our degree of adherence to these magnificent standards.

"Ever deepening humility, accompanied by an ever greater willingness to accept and to act upon clear-cut obligations—these are truly our touchstones for all growth in the life of the spirit. They hold up to us the very essence of right being and right doing. It is by them that we are enabled to find and to do God's will."

TALK, 1965 (PRINTED IN GRAPEVINE, JANUARY 1966)

Troubles of Our Own Making

Selfishness—self-centeredness! That, we think, is the root of our troubles. Driven by a hundred forms of fear, self-delusion, self-seeking, and self-pity, we step on the toes of our fellows and they retaliate. Sometimes they hurt us, seemingly without provocation, but we invariably find that at some time in the past we have made decisions based on self which later placed us in a position to be hurt.

So our troubles, we think, are basically of our own making. They arise out of ourselves, and the alcoholic is an extreme example of self-will run riot, though he usually doesn't think so. Above everything, we alcoholics must be rid of this selfishness. We must, or it kills us!

Compelling Love

The life of each A.A. and of each group is built around our Twelve Steps and Twelve Traditions. We know that the penalty for extensive disobedience to these principles is death for the individual and dissolution for the group. But an even greater force for A.A.'s unity is our compelling love for our fellow members and for our principles.

«« »»

You might think the people at A.A.'s headquarters in New York would surely have to have some personal authority. But, long ago, trustees and secretaries alike found they could do no more than make very mild suggestions to the A.A. groups.

They even had to coin a couple of sentences which still go into half the letters they write: "Of course you are at perfect liberty to handle this matter any way you please. But the majority experience in A.A. does seem to suggest . . ."

A.A. world headquarters is not a giver of orders. It is, instead, our largest transmitter of the lessons of experience.

1. TWELVE CONCEPTS, P. 8
2. TWELVE AND TWELVE, PP. 173–174

Going It Alone

Going it alone in spiritual matters is dangerous. How many times have we heard well-intentioned people claim the guidance of God when it was plain that they were mistaken? Lacking both practice and humility, they had deluded themselves and so were able to justify the most arrant nonsense on the ground that this was what God had told them.

People of very high spiritual development almost always insist on checking with friends or spiritual advisers the guidance they feel they have received from God. Surely, then, a novice ought not lay himself open to the chance of making foolish, perhaps tragic, blunders. While the comment or advice of others may not be infallible, it is likely to be far more specific than any direct guidance we may receive while we are still inexperienced in establishing contact with a Power greater than ourselves.

Recovery Through Giving

For a new prospect, outline the program of action, explaining how you made a self-appraisal, how you straightened out your past, and why you are now endeavoring to be helpful to him. It is important for him to realize that your attempt to pass this on to him plays a vital part in your own recovery. Actually, he may be helping you more than you are helping him. Make it plain that he is under no obligation to you.

« « «   » » »

In the first six months of my own sobriety, I worked hard with many alcoholics. Not a one responded. Yet this work kept me sober. It wasn't a question of those alcoholics giving me anything. My stability came out of trying to give, not out of demanding that I receive.

1. ALCOHOLICS ANONYMOUS, P. 94
2. GRAPEVINE, JANUARY 1958

A Higher Power for Atheists

"I have had many experiences with atheists, mostly good. Everybody in A.A. has the right to his own opinion. It is much better to maintain an open and tolerant society than it is to suppress any small disturbances their opinions might occasion. Actually, I don't know of anybody who went off and died of alcoholism because of some atheist's opinions on the cosmos.

"But I do always entreat these folks to look to a 'Higher Power'—namely, their own group. When they come in, most of their A.A. group is sober, and they are drunk. Therefore, the group is a 'Higher Power.' That's a good enough start, and most of them do progress from there. I know how they feel, because I was once that way myself."

LETTER, 1962

To Lighten Our Burden

Only one consideration should qualify our desire
for a complete disclosure of the damage we have
done. That will arise where a full revelation would
seriously harm the one to whom we are making
amends. Or—quite as important—other people.
We cannot, for example, unload a detailed account
of extramarital adventuring upon the shoulders
of our unsuspecting wife or husband.

It does not lighten our burden when we recklessly
make the crosses of others heavier.

《《《　》》》

In making amends, we should be sensible, tactful,
considerate, and humble without being servile or
scraping. As God's people, we stand on our
feet; we don't crawl before anyone.

1. TWELVE AND TWELVE, P. 86
2. ALCOHOLICS ANONYMOUS, P. 83

Speak Up Without Fear

Few of us are anonymous so far as our daily contacts go. We have dropped anonymity at this level because we think our friends and associates ought to know about A.A. and what it has done for us. We also wish to lose the fear of admitting that we are alcoholics. Though we earnestly request reporters not to disclose our identities, we frequently speak before semipublic gatherings. We wish to convince audiences that our alcoholism is a sickness we no longer fear to discuss before anyone.

If, however, we venture beyond this limit, we shall surely lose the principle of anonymity forever. If every A.A. felt free to publish his own name, picture, and story, we would soon be launched upon a vast orgy of personal publicity.

«« «   » »»

"While the so-called public meeting is questioned by many A.A. members, I favor it myself providing only that anonymity is respected in press reports and that we ask nothing for ourselves except understanding."

1. GRAPEVINE, JANUARY 1946
2. LETTER, 1949

The Fine Art of Alibis

The majority of A.A. members have suffered severely from self-justification during their drinking days. For most of us, self-justification was the maker of excuses for drinking and for all kinds of crazy and damaging conduct. We had made the invention of alibis a fine art.

We had to drink because times were hard or times were good. We had to drink because at home we were smothered with love or got none at all. We had to drink because at work we were great successes or dismal failures. We had to drink because our nation had won a war or lost a peace. And so it went, ad infinitum.

To see how our own erratic emotions victimized us often took a long time. Where other people were concerned, we had to drop the word "blame" from our speech and thought.

TWELVE AND TWELVE
1. PP. 46-47
2. P. 47

Spiritually Fit

Assuming we are spiritually fit, we can do all sorts
of things alcoholics are not supposed to do.
People have said we must not go where liquor is
served; we must not have it in our homes;
we must shun friends who drink; we must
avoid moving pictures which show drinking
scenes; we must not go into bars; our friends must
hide their bottles if we go to their houses; we
mustn't think or be reminded about alcohol at
all. Our experience shows that this is not
necessarily so.

We meet these conditions every day. An alcoholic
who cannot meet them still has an alcoholic mind;
there is something the matter with his spiritual
status. His only chance for sobriety would be
some place like the Greenland icecap, and even
there an Eskimo might turn up with a bottle of
Scotch and ruin everything!

ALCOHOLICS ANONYMOUS, PP. 100-101

Ourselves as Individuals

There is only one sure test of all spiritual experiences: "By their fruits, ye shall know them."

This is why I think we should question no one's transformation—whether it be sudden or gradual. Nor should we demand anyone's special type for ourselves, because experience suggests that we are apt to receive whatever may be the most useful for our own needs.

《《《　》》》

Human beings are never quite alike, so each of us, when making an inventory, will need to determine what his individual character defects are. Having found the shoes that fit, he ought to step into them and walk with new confidence that he is at last on the right track.

1. GRAPEVINE, JULY 1962
2. TWELVE AND TWELVE, P. 48

Instincts Run Wild

Every time a person imposes his instincts unreasonably upon others, unhappiness follows. If the pursuit of wealth tramples upon people who happen to be in the way, then anger, jealousy, and revenge are likely to be aroused. If sex runs riot, there is a similar uproar.

Demands made upon other people for too much attention, protection, and love can invite only domination or revulsion in the protectors themselves—two emotions quite as unhealthy as the demands which evoked them. When an individual's desire for prestige becomes uncontrollable, whether in the sewing circle or at the international conference table, other people suffer and often revolt. This collision of instincts can produce anything from a cold snub to a blazing revolution.

"Powerless over Alcohol"

I had gone steadily downhill, and on that day in 1934 I lay upstairs in the hospital, knowing for the first time that I was utterly hopeless.

Lois was downstairs, and Dr. Silkworth was trying in his gentle way to tell her what was wrong with me and that I was hopeless. "But Bill has a tremendous amount of will power," she said. "He has tried desperately to get well. We have tried everything. Doctor, why can't he stop?"

He explained that my drinking, once a habit, had become an obsession, a true insanity that condemned me to drink against my will.

«« »»

"In the late stages of our drinking, the will to resist has fled. Yet when we admit complete defeat and when we become entirely ready to try A.A. principles, our obsession leaves us and we enter a new dimension—freedom under God as we understand Him."

1. A.A. COMES OF AGE, P. 52
2. LETTER, 1966

Faith—a Blueprint—and Work

"The idea of 'twenty-four-hour living' applies primarily to the emotional life of the individual. Emotionally speaking, we must not live in yesterday, nor in tomorrow.

"But I have never been able to see that this means the individual, the group, or A.A. as a whole should give no thought whatever to how to function tomorrow or even in the more distant future. Faith alone never constructed the house you live in. There had to be a blueprint and a lot of work to bring it into reality.

"Nothing is truer for us of A.A. than the Biblical saying 'Faith without works is dead.' A.A.'s services, all designed to make more and better Twelfth Step work possible, are the 'works' that insure our life and growth by preventing anarchy or stagnation."

LETTER, 1954

False Pride

The alarming thing about pride-blindness is the ease with which it is justified. But we need not look far to see that self-justification is a universal destroyer of harmony and of love. It sets man against man, nation against nation. By it, every form of folly and violence can be made to look right, and even respectable.

«« « » »»

It would be a product of false pride to claim that A.A. is a cure-all, even for alcoholism.

1. GRAPEVINE, JUNE 1961
2. A.A. COMES OF AGE, P. 232

Mastering Resentments

We began to see that the world and its people
had really dominated us. Under that unhappy
condition, the wrongdoing of others, fancied or
real, had power to actually kill us, because we
could be driven back to drink through resentment. We saw that these resentments must be
mastered, but how? We could not wish them away.

This was our course: We realized that the people
who wronged us were perhaps spiritually sick.
So we asked God to help us show them the
same tolerance, pity, and patience that we would
cheerfully grant a sick friend.

Today, we avoid retaliation or argument. We
cannot treat sick people that way. If we do, we
destroy our chance of being helpful. We cannot be
helpful to all people, but at least God will show
us how to take a kindly and tolerant view of each
and every one.

ALCOHOLICS ANONYMOUS, PP. 66-67

Aspects of Spirituality

"Among A.A.'s there is still a vast amount of mix-up respecting what is material and what is spiritual. I prefer to believe that it is all a matter of motive. If we use our worldly possessions too selfishly, then we are materialists. But if we share these possessions in helpfulness to others, then the material aids the spiritual."

《 《 《   》 》 》

"The idea keeps persisting that the instincts are primarily bad and are the roadblocks before which all spirituality falters. I believe that the difference between good and evil is not the difference between spiritual and instinctual man; it is the difference between proper and improper use of the instinctual. Recognition and right channeling of the instinctual are the essence of achieving wholeness."

1. LETTER, 1958
2. LETTER, 1954

Emotional Sobriety

If we examine every disturbance we have, great or small, we will find at the root of it some unhealthy dependency and its consequent unhealthy demand. Let us, with God's help, continually surrender these hobbling liabilities.

Then we can be set free to live and love; we may then be able to twelfth-step ourselves, as well as others, into emotional sobriety.

When Conflicts Mount

Sometimes I would be forced to look at situations where I was doing badly. Right away, the search for excuses would become frantic.

"These," I would exclaim, "are really a good man's faults." When that pet gadget broke apart, I would think, "Well, if those people would only treat me right, I wouldn't have to behave the way I do." Next was this: "God well knows that I do have awful compulsions. I just can't get over this one. So He will have to release me." At last came the time when I would shout, "This, I positively will not do! I won't even try."

Of course, my conflicts went right on mounting, because I was simply loaded with excuses, refusals, and outright rebellion.

《《《　》》》

In self-appraisal, what comes to us alone may be garbled by our own rationalization and wishful thinking. The benefit of talking to another person is that we can get his direct comment and counsel on our situation.

1. GRAPEVINE, JUNE 1961
2. TWELVE AND TWELVE, P. 60

Time Versus Money

Our attitude toward the giving of time when compared with our attitude toward giving money presents an interesting contrast. We give a lot of our time to A.A. activities for our own protection and growth, but also for the sake of our groups, our areas, A.A. as a whole, and, above all, the newcomer. Translated into terms of money, these collective sacrifices would add up to a huge sum.

But when it comes to the actual spending of cash, particularly for A.A. service overhead, many of us are apt to turn a bit reluctant. We think of the loss of all that earning power in our drinking years, of those sums we might have laid by for emergencies or for education of the kids.

In recent years, this attitude is everywhere on the decline; it quickly disappears when the real need for a given A.A. service becomes clear. Donors can seldom see what the exact result has been. They well know, however, that countless thousands of other alcoholics and their families are being helped.

TWELVE CONCEPTS, PP. 63–64

Pain-Killer—or Pain-Healer

"I believe that when we were active alcoholics we drank mostly to kill pain of one kind or another—physical or emotional or psychic. Of course, everybody has a cracking point, and I suppose you reached yours—hence, the resort once more to the bottle.

"If I were you, I wouldn't heap devastating blame on myself for this; on the other hand, the experience should redouble your conviction that alcohol has no permanent value as a pain-killer."

««« »»»

In every A.A. story, pain has been the price of admission into a new life. But this admission price purchased more than we expected. It led us to a measure of humility, which we soon discovered to be a healer of pain. We began to fear pain less, and desire humility more than ever.

1. LETTER, 1959
2. TWELVE AND TWELVE, P. 75

Toward Partnership

When the distortion of family life through alcohol
has been great, a long period of patient striving
may be necessary. After the husband joins A.A.,
the wife may become discontented, even highly
resentful that A.A. has done the very thing
that all her years of devotion had failed to do.
Her husband may become so wrapped up in A.A.
and his new friends that he is inconsiderately
away from home more than when he drank. Each
then blames the other.

But eventually the alcoholic, now fully understanding how much he did to hurt his wife and
children, nearly always takes up his marriage
responsibilities with a willingness to repair what he
can and accept what he can't. He persistently
tries all of A.A.'s Twelve Steps in his home, often
with fine results. He firmly but lovingly commences to behave like a partner instead of like a
bad boy.

TWELVE AND TWELVE, PP. 118-119

Rebellion or Acceptance

All of us pass through times when we can pray
only with the greatest exertion. Occasionally we
go even further than this. We are seized with a
rebellion so sickening that we simply won't pray.
When these things happen, we should not think
too ill of ourselves. We should simply resume
prayer as soon as we can, doing what we know
to be good for us.

« « «   » » »

A man who persists in prayer finds himself in
possession of great gifts. When he has to deal
with hard circumstances, he finds he can face
them. He can accept himself and the world around
him.

He can do this because he now accepts a God
who is All—and who loves all. When he says,
"Our Father who art in heaven, hallowed be Thy
name," he deeply and humbly means it. When in
good meditation and thus freed from the clamors
of the world, he knows that he is in God's hands,
that his own ultimate destiny is really secure,
here and hereafter, come what may.

1. TWELVE AND TWELVE, P. 105
2. GRAPEVINE, JUNE 1958

Love + Rationality = Growth

"It seems to me that the primary object of any human being is to grow, as God intended, that being the nature of all growing things.

"Our search must be for what reality we can find, which includes the best definition and feeling of love that we can acquire. If the capability of loving is in the human being, then it must surely be in his Creator.

"Theology helps me in that many of its concepts cause me to believe that I live in a rational universe under a loving God, and that my own irrationality can be chipped away, little by little. This is, I suppose, the process of growth for which we are intended."

LETTER, 1958

Praying Rightly

We thought we had been deeply serious about religious practices. However, upon honest appraisal we found that we had been most superficial. Or sometimes, going to extremes, we had wallowed in emotionalism and had also mistaken this for true religious feeling. In both cases, we had been asking something for nothing.

We had not prayed rightly. We had always said, "Grant me my wishes," instead of "Thy will be done." The love of God and man we understood not at all. Therefore we remained self-deceived, and so incapable of receiving enough grace to restore us to sanity.

Daily Inventory

Often, as we review each day, only the closest scrutiny will reveal what our true motives were. There are cases where our ancient enemy rationalization has stepped in and has justified conduct which was really wrong. The temptation here is to imagine that we had good motives and reasons when we really hadn't.

We "constructively criticized" someone who needed it, when our real motive was to win a useless argument. Or, the person concerned not being present, we thought we were helping others to understand him, when in actuality our true motive was to feel superior by pulling him down.

We hurt those we loved because they needed to be "taught a lesson," but we really wanted to punish. We were depressed and complained we felt bad, when in fact we were mainly asking for sympathy and attention.

A Vision of the Whole

"Though many of us have had to struggle for sobriety, never yet has this Fellowship had to struggle for lost unity. Consequently, we sometimes take this one great gift for granted. We forget that, should we lose our unity, the millions of alcoholics who still 'do not know' might never get their chance."

《《《　》》》

"We used to be skeptical about large A.A. gatherings like conventions, thinking they might prove too exhibitionistic. But, on balance, their benefit is huge. While each A.A.'s interest should center principally in those about him and upon his own group, it is both necessary and desirable that we all get a larger vision of the whole.

"The General Service Conference in New York also produces this effect upon those who attend. It is a vision-stretching process."

1. LETTER, 1949
2. LETTER, 1956

A Mighty Beginning

Even the newest of newcomers finds undreamed rewards as he tries to help his brother alcoholic, the one who is even blinder than he. This is indeed the kind of giving that actually demands nothing. He does not expect his brother sufferer to pay him, or even to love him.

And then he discovers that through the divine paradox of this kind of giving he has found his own reward, whether or not his brother has yet received anything. His own character may still be gravely defective, but he somehow knows that God has enabled him to make a mighty beginning, and he senses that he stands at the edge of new mysteries, joys, and experiences of which he had never before dreamed.

Anonymity and Sobriety

As the A.A. groups multiplied, so did anonymity problems. Enthusiastic over the spectacular recovery of a brother alcoholic, we'd sometimes discuss those intimate and harrowing aspects of his case meant for his sponsor's ear alone. The aggrieved victim would then rightly declare that his trust had been broken.

When such stories got into circulation outside of A.A., the loss of confidence in our anonymity promise was severe. It frequently turned people from us. Clearly, every A.A. member's name—and story, too—had to be confidential, if he wished.

《《《　》》》

We now fully realize that 100 per cent personal anonymity before the public is just as vital to the life of A.A. as 100 per cent sobriety is to the life of each and every member. This is not the counsel of fear; it is the prudent voice of long experience.

1. TWELVE AND TWELVE, P. 185
2. A.A COMES OF AGE, P. 293

People of Faith

We who have traveled a path through agnosticism
or atheism beg you to lay aside prejudice, even
against organized religion. We have learned that,
whatever the human frailties of various faiths may
be, those faiths have given purpose and direction
to millions. People of faith have a rational idea
of what life is all about.

Actually, we used to have no reasonable conception whatever. We used to amuse ourselves by
cynically dissecting spiritual beliefs and practices,
when we might have seen that many spiritually-
minded persons of all races, colors, and
creeds were demonstrating a degree of stability,
happiness, and usefulness that we should have
sought for ourselves.

To Rebuild Security

In our behavior respecting financial and emotional security, fear, greed, possessiveness, and pride have too often done their worst. Surveying his business or employment record, almost any alcoholic can ask questions like these: In addition to my drinking problem, what character defects contributed to my financial instability? Did fear and inferiority about my fitness for my job destroy my confidence and fill me with conflict? Or did I overvalue myself and play the big shot?

Businesswomen in A.A. will find that these questions often apply to them, too, and the alcoholic housewife can also make the family financially insecure. Indeed, all alcoholics need to cross-examine themselves ruthlessly to determine how their own personality defects have demolished their security.

TWELVE AND TWELVE, PP. 51-52

Comradeship in Peril

We A.A.'s are like the passengers of a great liner the moment after rescue from shipwreck, when camaraderie, joyousness, and democracy pervade the vessel from steerage to captain's table.

Unlike the feelings of the ship's passengers, however, our joy in escape from disaster does not subside as we go our individual ways. The feeling of sharing in a common peril—relapse into alcoholism—continues to be an important element in the powerful cement which binds us of A.A. together.

«« »»

Our first woman alcoholic had been a patient of Dr. Harry Tiebout's, and he had handed her a prepublication manuscript copy of the Big Book. The first reading made her rebellious, but the second convinced her. Presently she came to a meeting held in our living room, and from there she returned to the sanitarium carrying this classic message to a fellow patient: "We aren't alone any more."

1. ALCOHOLICS ANONYMOUS, P. 17
2. A.A. COMES OF AGE, P. 18

Loving Advisers

Had I not been blessed with wise and loving advisers, I might have cracked up long ago. A doctor once saved me from death by alcoholism because he obliged me to face up to the deadliness of that malady. Another doctor, a psychiatrist, later on helped me save my sanity because he led me to ferret out some of my deep-lying defects. From a clergyman I acquired the truthful principles by which we A.A.'s now try to live.

But these precious friends did far more than supply me with their professional skills. I learned that I could go to them with any problem whatever. Their wisdom and their integrity were mine for the asking.

Many of my dearest A.A. friends have stood with me in exactly this same relation. Oftentimes they could help where others could not, simply because they were A.A.'s.

304

Single Purpose

There are those who predict that A.A. may well become a new spearhead for a spiritual awakening throughout the world. When our friends say these things, they are both generous and sincere. But we of A.A. must reflect that such a tribute and such a prophecy could well prove to be a heady drink for most of us—that is, if we really came to believe this to be the real purpose of A.A., and if we commenced to behave accordingly.

Our Society, therefore, will prudently cleave to its single purpose: the carrying of the message to the alcoholic who still suffers. Let us resist the proud assumption that since God has enabled us to do well in one area we are destined to be a channel of saving grace for everybody.

A.A. COMES OF AGE, P. 232

From the Taproot

The principle that we shall find no enduring strength until we first admit complete defeat is the main taproot from which our whole Society has sprung and flowered.

《《《　》》》

Every newcomer is told, and soon realizes for himself, that his humble admission of powerlessness over alcohol is his first step toward liberation from its paralyzing grip.

So it is that we first see humility as a necessity. But this is the barest beginning. To get completely away from our aversion to the idea of being humble, to gain a vision of humility as the avenue to true freedom of the human spirit, to be willing to work for humility as something to be desired for itself, takes most of us a long, long time. A whole lifetime geared to self-centeredness cannot be set in reverse all at once.

TWELVE AND TWELVE
1. PP. 21-22
2. PP. 72-73

Is Happiness the Goal?

"I don't think happiness or unhappiness is the point. How do we meet the problems we face? How do we best learn from them and transmit what we have learned to others, if they would receive the knowledge?

"In my view, we of this world are pupils in a great school of life. It is intended that we try to grow, and that we try to help our fellow travelers to grow in the kind of love that makes no demands. In short, we try to move toward the image and likeness of God as we understand Him.

"When pain comes, we are expected to learn from it willingly, and help others to learn. When happiness comes, we accept it as a gift, and thank God for it."

LETTER, 1950

Circle and Triangle

Above us, at the International Convention at
St. Louis in 1955, floated a banner on which was
inscribed the then new symbol for A.A., a circle
enclosing a triangle. The circle stands for the
whole world of A.A., and the triangle stands for
A.A.'s Three Legacies: Recovery, Unity, and
Service.

It is perhaps no accident that priests and seers of
antiquity regarded this symbol as a means of
warding off spirits of evil.

《《《　》》》

When, in 1955, we oldtimers turned over our
Three Legacies to the whole movement, nostalgia
for the old days blended with gratitude for the
great day in which I was now living. No more
would it be necessary for me to act for, decide for,
or protect A.A.

For a moment, I dreaded the coming change. But
this mood quickly passed. The conscience of A.A.
as moved by the guidance of God could be depended upon to insure A.A.'s future. Clearly my
job henceforth was to let go and let God.

A.A. COMES OF AGE
1. P. 139
2. PP. 46, 48

A Way Out of Depression

"During acute depression, avoid trying to set your whole life in order all at once. If you take on assignments so heavy that you are sure to fail in them at the moment, then you are allowing yourself to be tricked by your unconscious. Thus you will continue to make sure of your failure, and when it comes you will have another alibi for still more retreat into depression.

"In short, the 'all or nothing' attitude is a most destructive one. It is best to begin with whatever the irreducible minimums of activity are. Then work for an enlargement of these—day by day. Don't be disconcerted by setbacks—just start over."

LETTER, 1960

309

Spiritual Axiom

It is a spiritual axiom that every time we are
disturbed, no matter what the cause, there is
something wrong with us. If somebody hurts us
and we are sore, we are in the wrong, too.

But are there no exceptions to this rule? What
about "justifiable" anger? If somebody cheats us,
aren't we entitled to be mad? And shouldn't we
be properly angry with self-righteous folks?

For us of A.A. these adventures in anger are
sometimes very dangerous. We have found that
even justified anger ought to be left to those
better qualified to handle it.

Learning to Trust

Our entire A.A. program rests upon the principle of mutual trust. We trust God, we trust A.A., and we trust each other. Therefore, we trust our leaders in world service. The "Right of Decision" that we offer them is not only the practical means by which they may act and lead effectively, but it is also the symbol of our implicit confidence.

《《《 　》》》

If you arrive at A.A. with no religious convictions, you can, if you wish, make A.A. itself or even your A.A. group your "Higher Power." Here's a large group of people who have solved their alcohol problem. In this respect they are certainly a power greater than you. Even this minimum of faith will be enough.

Many members who have crossed the threshold just this way will tell you that, once across, their faith broadened and deepened. Relieved of the alcohol obsession, their lives unaccountably transformed, they came to believe in a Higher Power, and most of them began to talk of God.

1. TWELVE CONCEPTS, P. 16
2. TWELVE AND TWELVE, PP. 27–28

Telling the Worst

Though the variations were many, my main
theme was always "How godawful I am!" Just as
I often exaggerated my modest attainments by
pride, so I exaggerated my defects through guilt.
I would race about, confessing all (and a great
deal more) to whoever would listen. Believe it or
not, I took this widespread exposure of my sins
to be great humility on my part, and considered it
a great spiritual asset and consolation!

But later on I realized at depth that the great
harms I had done others were not truly regretted.
These episodes were merely the basis for story-
telling and exhibitionism. With this realization
came the beginning of a certain amount of
humility.

Tolerance Keeps Us Sober

"Honesty with ourselves and others gets us sober, but it is tolerance that keeps us that way.

"Experience shows that few alcoholics will long stay away from a group just because they don't like the way it is run. Most return and adjust themselves to whatever conditions they must. Some go to a different group, or form a new one.

"In other words, once an alcoholic fully realizes that he cannot get well alone, he will somehow find a way to get well and stay well in the company of others. It has been that way from the beginning of A.A. and probably always will be so."

LETTER, 1943

In the Sunlight at Last

When the thought was expressed that there might
be a God personal to me, I didn't like the idea.
So my friend Ebby made what then seemed a
novel suggestion. He said, "Why don't you choose
your own conception of God?"

That statement hit me hard. It melted the icy in-
tellectual mountain in whose shadow I had lived
and shivered many years. I stood in the sunlight
at last.

« « «   » » »

It may be possible to find explanations of spiritual
experiences such as ours, but I have often tried
to explain my own and have succeeded only in
giving the story of it. I know the feeling it gave me
and the results it has brought, but I realize I may
never fully understand its deeper why and how.

1. ALCOHOLICS ANONYMOUS, P. 12
2. A.A. COMES OF AGE, P. 45

High and Low

When our membership was small, we dealt with "low-bottom cases" only. Many less desperate alcoholics tried A.A., but did not succeed because they could not make the admission of their hopelessness.

In the following years, this changed. Alcoholics who still had their health, their families, their jobs, and even two cars in the garage, began to recognize their alcoholism. As this trend grew, they were joined by young people who were scarcely more than potential alcoholics. How could people such as these take the First Step?

By going back in our own drinking histories, we showed them that years before we realized it we were out of control, that our drinking even then was no mere habit, that it was indeed the beginning of a fatal progression.

Greater than Ourselves

If a mere code of morals or a better philosophy of life were sufficient to overcome alcoholism, many of us would have recovered long ago. But we found that such codes and philosophies did not save us, no matter how much we tried. We could wish to be moral, we could wish to be philosophically comforted, in fact, we could will these things with all our might, but the power needed for change wasn't there. Our human resources, as marshaled by the will, were not sufficient; they failed utterly.

Lack of power: That was our dilemma. We had to find a power by which we could live—and it had to be a Power greater than ourselves.

ALCOHOLICS ANONYMOUS, PP. 44-45

Our Protective Mantle

Almost every newspaper reporter who covers A.A. complains, at first, of the difficulty of writing his story without names. But he quickly forgets this difficulty when he realizes that here is a group of people who care nothing for acclaim.

Probably this is the first time in his life he has ever reported on an organization that wants no personalized publicity. Cynic though he may be, this obvious sincerity quickly transforms him into a friend of A.A.

《 《 《   》 》 》

Moved by the spirit of anonymity, we try to give up our natural desires for personal distinction as A.A. members, both among fellow alcoholics and before the general public. As we lay aside these very human aspirations, we believe that each of us takes part in the weaving of a protective mantle which covers our whole Society and under which we may grow and work in unity.

1. GRAPEVINE, MARCH 1946
2. TWELVE AND TWELVE, P. 187

Vision Beyond Today

Vision is, I think, the ability to make good estimates, both for the immediate and for the more distant future. Some might feel this sort of striving to be heresy against "One day at a time." But that valuable principle really refers to our mental and emotional lives and means chiefly that we are not foolishly to repine over the past nor wishfully to daydream about the future.

As individuals and as a fellowship, we shall surely suffer if we cast the whole job of planning for tomorrow onto a fatuous idea of providence. God's real providence has endowed us human beings with a considerable capability for foresight, and He evidently expects us to use it. Of course, we shall often miscalculate the future in whole or in part, but that is better than to refuse to think at all.

TWELVE CONCEPTS, P. 40

Forgiveness

Through the vital Fifth Step, we began to get the feeling that we could be forgiven, no matter what we had thought or done.

Often it was while working on this Step with our sponsors or spiritual advisers that we first felt truly able to forgive others, no matter how deeply we felt they had wronged us.

Our moral inventory had persuaded us that all-round forgiveness was desirable, but it was only when we resolutely tackled Step Five that we inwardly knew we'd be able to receive forgiveness and give it, too.

TWELVE AND TWELVE, PP. 57-58

Two Authorities

Many people wonder how A.A. can function under a seeming anarchy. Other societies have to have law and force and sanction and punishment, administered by authorized people. Happily for us, we found that we need no human authority whatever. We have two authorities which are far more effective. One is benign, the other malign.

There is God, our Father, who very simply says, "I am waiting for you to do my will." The other authority is named John Barleycorn, and he says, "You had better do God's will or I will kill you."

《《《　》》》

The A.A. Traditions are neither rules, regulations, nor laws. We obey them willingly because we ought to and because we want to. Perhaps the secret of their power lies in the fact that these life-giving communications spring out of living experience and are rooted in love.

1. A.A. COMES OF AGE, P. 105
2. A.A. TODAY, P. 11

320

Running the Whole Show

Most people try to live by self-propulsion. Each person is like an actor who wants to run the whole show and is forever trying to arrange the lights, the scenery, and the rest of the players in his own way. If his arrangements would only stay put, if only people would do as he wished, the show would be great.

What usually happens? The show doesn't come off very well. Admitting he may be somewhat at fault, he is sure that other people are more to blame. He becomes angry, indignant, self-pitying.

Is he not really a self-seeker even when trying to be useful? Is he not a victim of the delusion that he can wrest satisfaction and happiness out of this world if he only manages well?

ALCOHOLICS ANONYMOUS, PP. 60-61

Results of Prayer

As the doubter tries the process of prayer, he should begin to add up the results. If he persists, he will almost surely find more serenity, more tolerance, less fear, and less anger. He will acquire a quiet courage, the kind that isn't tension-ridden. He can look at "failure" and "success" for what these really are. Problems and calamity will begin to mean his instruction, instead of his destruction. He will feel freer and saner.

The idea that he may have been hypnotizing himself by autosuggestion will become laughable. His sense of purpose and of direction will increase. His anxieties will commence to fade. His physical health will be likely to improve. Wonderful and unaccountable things will start to happen. Twisted relations in his family and on the outside will improve surprisingly.

GRAPEVINE, JUNE 1958

Easy Does It—but Do It

Procrastination is really sloth in five syllables.

《《《　》》》

"My observation is that some people can get by with a certain amount of postponement, but few can live with outright rebellion."

《《《　》》》

"We have succeeded in confronting many a problem drinker with that awful alternative, 'This we A.A.'s do, or we die.' Once this much is firmly in his mind, more drinking only turns the coil tighter.

"As many an alcoholic has said, 'I came to the place where it was either into A.A. or out the window. So here I am!' "

1. TWELVE AND TWELVE, P. 67
2. LETTER, 1952
3. LETTER, 1950

Groping Toward God

"More than most people, I think, alcoholics want to know who they are, what this life is about, whether they have a divine origin and an appointed destiny, and whether there is a system of cosmic justice and love.

"It is the experience of many of us in the early stages of drinking to feel that we have had glimpses of the Absolute and a heightened feeling of identification with the cosmos. While these glimpses and feelings doubtless have a validity, they are deformed and finally swept away in the chemical, spiritual, and emotional damage wrought by the alcohol itself.

"In A.A., and in many religious approaches, alcoholics find a great deal more of what they merely glimpsed and felt while trying to grope their way toward God in alcohol."

LETTER, 1960

Spirituality and Money

Some of us still ask, "Just what is this Third Legacy business anyhow? And just how much territory does 'service' take in?"

Let's begin with my own sponsor, Ebby. When Ebby heard how serious my drinking was, he resolved to visit me. He was in New York; I was in Brooklyn. His resolve was not enough; he had to take action and he had to spend money.

He called me on the phone and then got into the subway; total cost, ten cents. At the level of the telephone booth and subway turnstile, spirituality and money began to mix. One without the other would have amounted to nothing at all.

Right then and there, Ebby established the principle that A.A. in action calls for the sacrifice of much time and a little money.

Humility Brings Hope

Now that we no longer patronize bars and bordellos, now that we bring home the pay checks, now that we are so very active in A.A., and now that people congratulate us on these signs of progress—well, we naturally proceed to congratulate ourselves. Of course, we are not yet within hailing distance of humility.

《《《   》》》

We ought to be willing to try humility in seeking the removal of our other shortcomings, just as we did when we admitted that we were powerless over alcohol, and came to believe that a Power greater than ourselves could restore us to sanity.

If humility could enable us to find the grace by which the deadly alcohol obsession could be banished, then there must be hope of the same result respecting any other problem we can possibly have.

1. GRAPEVINE, JUNE 1961
2. TWELVE AND TWELVE, P. 76

Welcome Criticism

"Thanks much for your letter of criticism. I'm certain that had it not been for its strong critics, A.A. would have made slower progress.

"For myself, I have come to set a high value on the people who have criticized me, whether they have seemed reasonable critics or unreasonable ones. Both have often restrained me from doing much worse than I actually have done. The unreasonable ones have taught me, I hope, a little patience. But the reasonable ones have always done a great job for all of A.A.— and have taught me many a valuable lesson."

LETTER, 1955

Three Choices

The immediate object of our quest is sobriety—freedom from alcohol and from all its baleful consequences. Without this freedom, we have nothing at all.

Paradoxically, though, we can achieve no liberation from the alcohol obsession until we become willing to deal with those character defects which have landed us in that helpless condition. In this freedom quest, we are always given three choices.

A rebellious refusal to work upon our glaring defects can be an almost certain ticket to destruction. Or, perhaps for a time, we can stay sober with a minimum of self-improvement and settle ourselves into a comfortable but often dangerous mediocrity. Or, finally, we can continuously try hard for those sterling qualities that can add up to fineness of spirit and action—true and lasting freedom under God.

A New-Found Providence

When dealing with a prospect of agnostic or
atheistic bent, you had better use everyday
language to describe spiritual principles. There is
no use arousing any prejudice he may have against
certain theological terms and conceptions, about
which he may already be confused. Don't raise
such issues, no matter what your own convictions are.

«« «   » » »

Every man and woman who has joined A.A. and
intends to stick has, without realizing it, made a
beginning on Step Three. Isn't it true that, in all
matters touching upon alcohol, each of them
has decided to turn his or her life over to the
care, protection, and guidance of A.A.?

Already a willingness has been achieved to cast
out one's own will and one's own ideas about the
alcohol problem in favor of those suggested by
A.A. Now if this is not turning one's will and
life over to a new-found "Providence," then
what is it?

1. ALCOHOLICS ANONYMOUS, P. 93
2. TWELVE AND TWELVE, P. 35

Do It Our Way?

In praying, our immediate temptation will be to ask for specific solutions to specific problems, and for the ability to help other people as we have already thought they should be helped. In that case, we are asking God to do it our way. Therefore, we ought to consider each request carefully to see what its real merit is.

Even so, when making specific requests, it will be well to add to each one of them this qualification: ". . . if it be Thy will."

To Grow Up

Those adolescent urges that so many of us have for complete approval, utter security, and perfect romance—urges quite appropriate to age seventeen—prove to be an impossible way of life at forty-seven or fifty-seven.

Since A.A. began, I've taken huge wallops in all these areas because of my failure to grow up, emotionally and spiritually.

« « «   » » »

As we grow spiritually, we find that our old attitudes toward our instinctual drives need to undergo drastic revisions. Our demands for emotional security and wealth, for personal prestige and power all have to be tempered and redirected.

We learn that the full satisfaction of these demands cannot be the sole end and aim of our lives. We cannot place the cart before the horse, or we shall be pulled backward into disillusionment. But when we are willing to place spiritual growth first—then and only then do we have a real chance to grow in healthy awareness and mature love.

1. GRAPEVINE, JANUARY 1958
2. TWELVE AND TWELVE, P. 114

The Great Fact

We realize we know only a little. God will constantly disclose more to you and to us. Ask Him in your morning meditation what you can do each day for the man who is still sick. The answers will come, if your own house is in order.

But obviously you cannot transmit something you haven't got. See to it that your relationship with Him is right, and great events will come to pass for you and countless others. This is the great fact for us.

To the Newcomer:
Abandon yourself to God as you understand God. Admit your faults to Him and to your fellows. Clear away the wreckage of your past. Give freely of what you find and join us. We shall be with you in the fellowship of the spirit, and you will surely meet some of us as you trudge the road of happy destiny.

May God bless you and keep you—until then.

ALCOHOLICS ANONYMOUS, P. 164

I Am Responsible . . .

When anyone, anywhere, reaches out for help,
I want the hand of A.A. always to be there.
And for that: I am responsible.

—DECLARATION OF 30TH ANNIVERSARY
INTERNATIONAL CONVENTION, 1965

《 《 《　　》 》 》

DEAR FRIENDS:

Since 1938, the greatest part of my A.A. life has been spent in helping to create, design, manage, and insure the solvency and effectiveness of A.A.'s world services—the office of which has enabled our Fellowship to function all over the globe, and as a unified whole.

It is no exaggeration to say that, under their trustees, these all important services have accounted for much of our present size and over-all effectiveness.

The A.A. General Service Office is by far the largest single carrier of the A.A. message. It has well related A.A. to the troubled world in which we live. It has fostered the spread of our Fellowship everywhere. A.A. World Services, Inc., stands ready to serve the special needs of any group or isolated individual, no matter the distance or language. Its many years of accumulated experience are available to us all.

The members of our trusteeship—the General Service Board of A.A.—will, in the future, be our *primary leaders in all of our world affairs*. This high responsibility has long since been delegated to them; they are the successors in world service to Dr. Bob and to me, and they are directly accountable to A.A. as a whole.

This is the legacy of world-service responsibility that we vanishing oldtimers are leaving to you, the A.A.'s of today and tomorrow. We know that you will guard, support, and cherish this world legacy as the greatest collective responsibility that A.A. has or ever can have.

Yours in trust, and in affection,

Bill

Bill W. died on January 24, 1971.

THE TWELVE STEPS

1—We admitted we were powerless over alcohol—that our lives had become unmanageable.

2—Came to believe that a Power greater than ourselves could restore us to sanity.

3—Made a decision to turn our will and our lives over to the care of God *as we understood Him.*

4—Made a searching and fearless moral inventory of ourselves.

5—Admitted to God, to ourselves, and to another human being the exact nature of our wrongs.

6—Were entirely ready to have God remove all these defects of character.

7—Humbly asked Him to remove our shortcomings.

8—Made a list of all persons we had harmed, and became willing to make amends to them all.

9—Made direct amends to such people wherever possible, except when to do so would injure them or others.

10—Continued to take personal inventory and when we were wrong, promptly admitted it.

11—Sought through prayer and meditation to improve our conscious contact with God *as we understood Him,* praying only for knowledge of His will for us and the power to carry that out.

12—Having had a spiritual awakening as the result of these steps, we tried to carry this message to alcoholics and to practice these principles in all our affairs.

THE TWELVE TRADITIONS

1—Our common welfare should come first; personal recovery depends upon A.A. unity.

2—For our group purpose there is but one ultimate authority—a loving God as He may express Himself in our group conscience. Our leaders are but trusted servants; they do not govern.

3—The only requirement for A.A. membership is a desire to stop drinking.

4—Each group should be autonomous except in matters affecting other groups or A.A. as a whole.

5—Each group has but one primary purpose—to carry its message to the alcoholic who still suffers.

6—An A.A. group ought never endorse, finance or lend the A.A. name to any related facility or outside enterprise, lest problems of money, property and prestige divert us from our primary purpose.

7—Every A.A. group ought to be fully self-supporting, declining outside contributions.

8—Alcoholics Anonymous should remain forever non-professional, but our service centers may employ special workers.

9—A.A., as such, ought never be organized; but we may create service boards or committees directly responsible to those they serve.

10—Alcoholics Anonymous has no opinion on outside issues; hence the A.A. name ought never be drawn into public controversy.

11—Our public relations policy is based on attraction rather than promotion; we need always maintain personal anonymity at the level of press, radio and films.

12—Anonymity is the spiritual foundation of all our traditions, ever reminding us to place principles before personalities.